YEHUDI MENUHIN MUSIC GUIDES

Available
Violin and viola by Yehudi Menuhin and William Primrose
Piano by Louis Kentner
Clarinet by Jack Brymer

In preparation
contributions on
Bassoon by William Waterhouse
Double bass by John Gray
'Cello by Pierre Fournier
Flute by James Galway
Guitar and lute by Narciso Yepes
Harp by Sidonie Goossens
Horn by Barry Tuckwell
Organ by Simon Preston
Percussion by James Holland
Trombone by Alan Lumsden
Trumpet by Sidney Ellison
Tuba by John Fletcher

To follow
contributions on
Conducting and orchestration
Harpsichord and early keyboard instruments
Voice

YEHUDI MENUHIN MUSIC GUIDES

Oboe

Leon Goossens and
Edwin Roxburgh

SCHIRMER BOOKS
A Division of Macmillan Publishing Co., Inc.
NEW YORK

Schirmer Books
A Division of Macmillan Publishing Co., Inc.
866 Third Avenue, New York, N.Y. 10022

First American Edition 1977

Library of Congress Catalog Card Number: 77–15886

Printed in the United States of America

printing number

1 2 3 4 5 6 7 8 9 10

Library of Congress Cataloging in Publication Data

Goossens, Leon
    Oboe.

    (Yehudi Menuhin music guides)
    Bibliography: p.
    Discography: p.
    Includes index.
    1. Oboe--Instruction and study. I. Roxburgh, Edwin,
joint author.
MT360.G66   788'.7'07   77-15886
ISBN 0-02-871450-4
ISBN 0-02-871460-1 pbk.

Contents

EDITOR'S INTRODUCTION BY YEHUDI MENUHIN xi
AUTHORS' PREFACES xiii
INTRODUCTION 1

PART ONE HISTORY
Chapter One EARLY HISTORY UP TO 1800 5
Other members of the family: Alto oboe 15
Tenor oboe 15
Chapter Two INTRODUCTION OF THE MECHANIZED OBOE 17
The Bass oboe and Heckelphone 26

PART TWO THE REED AND THE OBOIST
Chapter Three THE REED 31
Reed making equipment 32
Gouging 37
Shaping 38
Binding 40
Scraping 42
Cor Anglais reeds 48
Oboe D'Amore reeds 49
Chapter Four GENERAL ASPECTS OF MODERN TECHNIQUES 50
Maintenance 50
The teacher 53
Producing the first sound 53
Embouchure 54
Posture 58
Scales 69
Breath control 70
Inhaling 72
Articulation and attack 76
Dynamics 81

	Tone quality	86
	Vibrato	87
	Tone quality of the Cor Anglais	93

PART THREE   THE MUSIC

Chapter Five	PLAYING BAROQUE MUSIC	97
	(by Edwin Roxburgh)	
	The problem	97
	Tone quality	98
	Henry Purcell	100
	Modern editions	102
	Style	103
	Ornaments	107
Chapter Six	PLAYING CLASSICAL MUSIC	134
	Inserting a cadenza	140
	Classical orchestral technique	143
Chapter Seven	PLAYING ROMANTIC MUSIC	149
Chapter Eight	20TH CENTURY MUSIC	158
	The rise of the solo oboist	158
	Recording	161
	Orchestral considerations	163
Chapter Nine	THE CONTEMPORARY WORLD	166
	(by Edwin Roxburgh)	
	Embouchure and reed	167
	Single sounds	170
	Multiphonic procedures	177
	Homogeneous chords	178
	Homogeneous chords mixed with	
	single notes	179
	Double harmonics	179
	Electronics and general considerations	181
APPENDICES	Appendix I: list of manufacturers	185
	Appendix II: the oboe repertoire	186
	Appendix III: fingering charts	211
BRIEF BIBLIOGRAPHY		216
BRIEF DISCOGRAPHY		221
INDEX		233

List of Plates

Plate numbers 1–4 between pages 32 and 33

One   a) Musicians from the Tomb of the
Leopards, Tarquinia
b) The Aulos player (*Courtesy of the Trustees
of the British Museum*)

Two   a) Musette (*Courtesy of the Royal College
of Music*)
b) Shawm (*Courtesy of the Horniman
Museum, London*)
c) Baroque oboe (*Courtesy of the Horniman
Museum, London*)
d) Curved Cor Anglais (*Courtesy of the
Horniman Museum, London*)

Three   a) Classical oboe: W. Milhouse, c. 1785
b) Classical oboe: Noblet frères, c. 1800
(*Finchcock collection*)
c) Oboe: Lorée, 1907
d) Oboe: Lorée, 1975
e) Oboe D'Amore: Louis, 1925
f) Cor Anglais: Rigoutat, 1950

Four   a) Tenor oboe: M. Lot, c. 1775
b) Bass (Baritone) oboe: Triebert, 1825
c) Cor Anglais, curved: C. Golde, 1840
d) Oboe: Tabard, c. 1830
(*All courtesy of the Royal College of Music*)

Plate numbers 5–8 between pages 64 and 65

Five   Reed-making equipment

Six   Equipment for gouging and shaping cane

Seven   The pre-gouging process

Eight   The gouging process and scraping

Plate numbers 9–12 between pages 128 and 129

Nine   a) The micrometre
         b) Five stages in cane preparation

Ten   The finished reed against the light

Eleven   Embouchure

Twelve   Correct posture

Plate numbers 13–16 between pages 160 and 161

Thirteen   Use of wrist between a″ and g″

Fourteen   18th century copy of a Purcell Ode
                     (*Courtesy of the Royal College of Music*)
Fifteen   Letter to Leon Goossens from Sir
                     Edward Elgar
Sixteen   Leon Goossens with Finnish students

ACKNOWLEDGEMENTS

Editorial board:

General editor: Yehudi Menuhin

Coordinating editor: Patrick Jenkins

Advisers: Martin Cooper
                         Eric Fenby
                         Robert Layton
                         Denis Stevens

Drawings: Tony Matthews

Photographs: Ian Dickson

Music examples: Malcolm Lipkin

The photographs of instruments in the museum of the Royal College of Music and the Purcell ms. (Plate 14) are reproduced by kind permission of the Director. The authors and publisher wish to thank Mr George A. Ingram and the staff of T. W. Howarth, London, for providing information and advice on technical matters. They are also grateful to Miss Barbara Banner for her help in collating the information in the repertoire section, and Mrs Leslie Goossens for her warm hospitality during the collaboration.

Editor's Introduction
by Yehudi Menuhin

It is with great pride and pleasure that I am introducing in our series of Music Guides this book on the oboe by Leon Goossens and Edwin Roxburgh. It joins the books which have already appeared in the completeness, the emotional attachment and the analytical objectivity which it brings to its subject.

I have known Leon Goossens since I was a boy and have made music with him many times. He is a great musician and one who is a master not only of his instrument but of the oboe's musical heritage as well.

Edwin Roxburgh among all young British composers has been most dear to me. He has not only travelled with my orchestra all over the world, but has also been our 'house' composer, arranging *Waltzing Matilda* in Australia for a farewell concert and composing music for television productions when my wife Diana read poems by Lear and e. e. cummings chosen by her and Edwin.

Both Leon and Edwin have handled the oboe from every angle, from the basic physical teaching and the stance to the fingering, the interpretation and the quality of sound. I am sure this is the book for which not only oboists have been waiting, but also those serious concert-goers who want to understand more about the instruments they enjoy.

YEHUDI MENUHIN,
1977

Authors' Prefaces

My initial reaction to Yehudi Menuhin's invitation for me to write this book was one of hesitation, until I understood the true intention of the series. Instead of a factual book of information here is a marvellous opportunity to translate my long experience of music into words for those who have shared with me its joy, whether through recordings, concerts or playing. I have endeavoured to inform the listener and the player, while thinking also of the young beginner and the interested parents who, through this book, may come even closer to the warmth and adventure which music can give. It has always been a great inspiration to make music with Yehudi. This book extends that experience into the secrets behind those performances.

LÉON GOOSSENS

In collaborating in the preparation of this book, the intention of the authors has been to provide a broader picture of the oboe than is generally considered necessary.

The name of Leon Goossens is synonymous with the oboe – an artist who has transformed the sound of an 'ill wind that no-one blows good' into a rapturous singer, leaving the mark of innovation on its future evolution. As an oboe-playing composer, it has been an experience of great pleasure and satisfaction to have worked with such a master.

We both share the view that oboe playing is a life-long adventure that never ceases to open new frontiers of awareness in the triangular relationship of listener, player and composer.

Our purpose has been to explain the instrument as an historical force in music; to provide a guide to its technique, and to lead the music lover through the mountain of music the oboe has inspired through the ages.

EDWIN ROXBURGH

A Note on Pitches

To avoid unnecessary musical examples the following pitch references are used, in accordance with a generally-accepted formula:

Introduction

It is easy for one who has spent his entire life as an oboist to revere the instrument with special favour within the woodwind family. Nevertheless, personal bias cannot change the fact that the oboe is the most ancient of the reed instruments, having evolved to its present design without any radical changes. An awareness of its long history is essential to a true understanding of the nature of the modern instrument, because, more than any other, the sound is highly personal and individualistic. Oboists make their own mouthpiece, which is never quite the same from performance to performance; also, they must maintain the mechanism with great care. Only when these two conditions are satisfied can they begin to make music. Therefore, it is the combined skills of the carpenter, the mechanic and the musician which produce an oboist. Seen in this light we may better understand Mozart's amazement at the unusual virtuosity of Ramm; or why Rossini, doubting the quality of English players, brought his own oboist to England for performances of his operas; or the qualities of a player like Gleditsch, who inspired all the obbligati in Bach's Cantatas and Passions.

Schools of technique and sound are less evident today than in the past – no doubt a situation created by the speed of communication on our shrinking 'global village'. The general nature of oboe tone quality has, however, changed enormously throughout the ages. It is no matter of conjecture, therefore, that a large part of the oboe repertoire, both solo and orchestral, has been created by the influence of individual players like Gleditsch and Ramm. In other words, it is not always the composer who has necessarily extended the expressive and technical range of the instrument at his own whim, so much as the individual players who have demonstrated uncatalogued skills to the composer. This is an important part of the mystique of the instrument which echoes back through the centuries before the symbolic paeans made to the Greek gods and Pan's immortal laments to Syrinx.

Part One

History

One

Early History up to 1800

> On the bed of Fate he lies, he rises not. The
> standing are not silent, the sitting are not silent,
> they set up a lament; his beloved concubine, his
> musician, his beloved entertainer . . .

So reads an ancient cuneiform tablet in the University
Museum of Philadelphia which describes a Sumerian royal
funeral. Curt Sachs suggests that some of these musicians
may well have been oboists because the geminated (or
double) pipes depicted in musical scenes are divergent – a
characteristic of most ancient oboes. Two examples excavated
by Sir Leonard Woolley at Ur form a pair almost identical
to later Egyptian oboes. They are the earliest oboes we know,
dating from 2800 B.C. We know very little about them
beyond speculation.

Our feet rest on firmer ground when we consider the Brah-
min epoch in India, from the twelfth to the seventh centuries
B.C. They used an instrument called the otou/ottu, a trans-
literation which sounds very like our own English oboe of
today. Like many ancient instruments it was conical, but
it was distinguished by the absence of finger-holes. The reed
was shaped like an equilateral triangle of $\frac{3}{8}$in. Like all
traditional instruments the otou has maintained its place
through tens of centuries and is still used today in ceremonial
dances. The player holds the instrument in his left hand and
can sustain the sound indefinitely by inhaling through his
nose. With his right hand he beats on a drum strapped to his
belt. Berlioz writes a rather bigoted description of the leader
of a troop of musicians from Calcutta who were visiting
Paris for the Great Exhibition. 'There was a wind instrument
something like our oboes, with a double reed and a tube
without holes which produces only one note. This primitive
oboe was used by the leader of the musicians who accompanied the Calcutta dancing-girls in Paris a few years ago.

He made an A drone on for hours on end, and those who like this note certainly got their money's worth.'

As a drone instrument it was used with the nagasuram, a larger instrument. Another kind was the sanayi, two of which were often joined together at an angle to form a double oboe. There were many varieties of reed instruments in India but with the exception of the otou and nagasuram we have very little knowledge of them.

Oboes were developed and used for ceremonial purposes in various forms throughout the ancient world, some of which have perpetuated the same characteristics up to the present day. Burmese and Mongolian instruments are long straight trumpets with flaring bells played with a very stiff reed. Chinese instruments are similar to Indian types. The Emperor Kang-Hi leaves us a written record of instruments used in China which describes an oboe called 'koan'; a single reed gave it the sonority of a small child's cry. Large ones had eight holes; seven on the front and one for the right-hand thumb. An interesting feature of these instruments is that they were held, contrary to present-day practice, with the right hand above the left. Today it is still possible to find various primitive kinds of instruments like these in Mexico.

In Egypt the oboe was a late-comer, being introduced during the New Kingdom about the fifteenth century B.C. Although ancient manuscripts do not show oboes, we may presume from the drums and clappers used by women dancers on reliefs of this period that oboes must have made a rather raucous music.

It is impossible to provide definitive conclusions about the music these instruments played. Neumes do appear on ancient manuscripts and papyri, and many scholars have provided exciting evidence for their interpretations. But, like the Etruscan or Mayan languages, many problems remain unanswered, and it would be foolish to claim authenticity for any decipherments beyond the vision of conjecture. Before the twentieth century, scientific research and assessment could lend little help to musicologists. Verdi showed a very fashionable 'infection with the antique' when he composed 'Aida'; an experience which left him with little patience for ill-founded theories on the subject of ancient Egyptian music. After being bridled into examining an ancient Egyptian flute by Fétis, the dogmatic musical *littérateur*, who claimed to have discovered the key to Egyptian modes with a reconstruction of the instrument, Verdi wrote to a friend:

'Do not think that I abhor this charlatan because he has run me down, but because one day he rushed me head over heels to the Egyptian Museum in Florence, to inspect a pipe on which he pretends to have discovered the system of the ancient Egyptian music, as he asserts in his "History of Music" . . . The archrogue!!! Thus history is falsified, and fools grow without watering!'

Although their music is shrouded with uncertainties, the ancients do provide much evidence for the structure and intonation of their instruments. This is mostly true of the Greeks and Romans who developed dozens of wind instruments which can be classified into two major categories: the Greek auloi (Roman equivalent, tibiae) and syrinx (Roman equivalent, fistulae). Homer provides the best clue to the nature of these categories when we read in the 'Iliad':

'When he (Agamemnon) gazed on the plains of Troy, he was astonished to see all those fires which were gleaming on the walls of Ilium and to hear the sound of the auloi and syrinx mingling with the noise of the crowd.'

The Greco-Roman characterization of the auloi as reed instruments and the syrinx as a flute (what we would call a flute-à-bec) is further emphasized when Aristotle writes about the double reed, or 'zengos', as the Greeks described it:

'The zenge (reeds) of the auloi must be compact, smooth and uniform, in order that the column of air which passes through them may also be smooth, uniform and uninterrupted. That is why the *zenge moistened with saliva* have a more mellow tone, while, when dry, they have a coarse tone, for the air which traverses a moist, smooth body is soft and uniform. The proof is that the breath itself, when it is moist, will strike less hard against the zenge and be dispersed, but if dry, it will adhere to the reed and make the attack rougher.'

What better reasoning could we offer an oboist today? We need no more proof than this to show that the aulos was an oboe played with a reed very much the same as we use now, although coarser and larger. Theophrastus goes further to explain the kind of cane used by the Greek aulos player:

'There are said to be two kinds of cane: the one for the wind instruments (auletic) and the other . . . they say, and it seems to be true, that when the water in Lake Orchomenus is higher the cane attains its full length the first year, but that it does not arrive at maturity until the following year if the water remains at the same level.'

He describes the foliage of the cane, explaining the uses for the various tubes, stating that the specimens which have no foliage (called eunuchs) are best for reeds:

'They claim that these are the best for the zenge, but that very few turn out well in the making.'

It seems that the Greek players had exactly the same kinds of problems as today's oboists! Emphasizing the advice Aristotle provides on moistening the reed, it seems that the connection between the ancient and modern instruments becomes closer and closer. We even have information concerning professional Greek reed-makers.

Classical literature abounds in discussions of the aulos and syrinx. Most museums contain Greek amphorae with illustrations of musicians and players. Perhaps one of the finest representations of the aulos-player is in the fresco of The Tomb of the Leopards **(plate 1).** The Etruscans were Greek in culture and the pipes shown here are very characteristic. The most immediately striking aspect is that the player has two pipes in his mouth, blowing both at the same time. They are divided (geminated) and each pipe is played with a single hand. Other kinds of aulos were used: pairs of parallel pipes and a single pipe (monaulos). But the most common were the double pipes which the Etruscan is playing. Anthony Baines has provided an excellent description of the Elgin pipes in the British Museum, the only examples of complete instruments that have survived from Greek classical times. The trials which Baines has made on replicas of these pipes provide some very sound theory on the tuning and technique of the aulos, which he describes as pentatonic: A, C, D, F (or E), G, A. Although the pipes usually had four holes, the lowest was left open, the little finger being occupied with holding up the instrument from underneath. The Etruscan player is especially interesting because the artist has managed to achieve good perspective in showing the blown-out cheeks of the player. Full lung-pressure was required; so much so that a kind of leather muzzle ('phorbeia') had to be worn, supporting the cheeks and covering the mouth, leaving an opening wide enough for the lips to form an embouchure. These varied enormously, as did the tone of different players. They were important enough for Sophocles to show anger when bellows were introduced to sustain the tone:

'They no longer blow in small auloi, but into terrible bellows and without bandages.'

This was a damning statement because, in common with all Greeks, Sophocles had a great admiration for the aulos and attached great importance to its function in life. Socrates also avers:

'Let us admit that a man, without being a good auletes, may wish to pass for such, should he not imitate the good auletes in exterior things. For the auletes has the habit of appearing in great pomp, followed by numerous servants. And because the good auletes is praised by many people, the other should surround himself with admirers. But he must never risk a public performance if he does not wish to make himself ridiculous and to be recognised as a wretched auletes and a man to be disdained.'

There is no doubt that it was an instrument of high virtuosity and sensitivity, used on all ceremonial occasions. Aristotle admitted that it aroused 'impetuous and passionate sensations in the soul'. In the days of the Empire the Romans too used it widely, especially on funereal occasions. According to reliefs and other representations little or no difference can be seen. They must have been kept sacred to at least one deity at Pompeii, for we have a perfectly preserved set of auloi rescued from the ruins which can now be seen at the Museo Nazionale at Naples. Several of them have the flared bell like the instrument played by the Etruscan at Tarquinia **(plate 1).**

Statius gives us an idea of the function of the larger instruments:

> 'The tibia with the curving end,
> Wont to lead the funeral rites of tender shades,
> Sounds a deep note.'

We can trace no significant development of the oboe in Western Europe from this time to the Late Middle Ages. As the Roman Empire declined, history made no reference to instrumental developments, and the Dark Ages found musical activity pressed into enclosed local cultures. Indeed, without the writings of Boethius and Cassiodorus the transmission of any knowledge of ancient Greek music to the Middle Ages could not have been possible. The oboe family survived mainly through the bands of travelling musicians, minstrels, troubadours and Town Guilds. Eventually, as a result of the Crusades, we discover that the line of evolution is not broken at all. At the time of the Arab occupation of Persia in the second half of the seventh century an intermingling of the two cultures produced the Arabian oboe, which was of Persian origin. This is the zamr, or surna, derived directly from the Persian shawm. The characteristics of this instrument are very close indeed to the early oboe. The reed is tied to a metal staple and, roughly speaking, the bore continues straight from the larger lower end. There is a wide flared bell. There were variations in the proportions, but all were between 312mm and 583mm long, with a range of $2\frac{1}{3}$ octaves to 3 octaves. The instrument was made of a single piece of cherry wood. The neck had a movable metal disc against which the player pressed his lips. This indicates that the reed was completely inserted into the mouth. It was capable of a vast range of expression and dextrous articulation. The Turks used it mainly for military band purposes such as weddings and warfare. It found its way to Europe with the returning Crusaders who brought the music of the Saracens with them.

The windbag variant of the Greek aulos (hated by Sophocles) is a constant partner to the mouth-blown instrument throughout history. Baines describes this as a 'folk-shawm' and lays stress on its importance as the essential correlative to the eventual union of the two kinds in the modern oboe. This view is determined by the fact that bagpipes in all cultures had no disc at the top of the instrument. The author has had some personal experience of playing this 'folk-shawm' or bagpipe when he appeared in a Welsh folk music festival, inscribed in the programme as 'Leon Goossens, Oboe and Pibgorn'. The name means 'horned chalumeau' (bagpipe), deriving from the two large horns at the end, one of which is hollowed out to form a bell; the other end holds a double reed. It makes a rich hollow sound, rather like a baroque cor anglais. The islanders of Anglesey have a tune called 'Pibgorn'. They dance to it with the accompaniment of this instrument.

Other examples of the windbag oboe were used for folk-dancing in the Middle Ages and the Renaissance. Pieter Brueghel the Elder provides marvellous representations of these occasions in paintings such as The Peasant Dance and The Peasant Wedding, which show bagpipe players leading the music. Judging from my own experience as a pibgorn-player, it was just as much fun and delight as it appears in the paintings. Varieties of these instruments include pommers, bombardons, chalumeaux and musettes. They had a small range not exceeding $1\frac{1}{2}$ octaves. But the deep, reedy sound was perfect for the dancing around the green during village festivals.

The emancipation of the artistic spirit in the Renaissance was reflected with incredible inventiveness in the field of woodwind instruments. A flowering of all the streams of development converged on Europe and literally hundreds of instruments flourished in the Courts, in the Military Academies and in the Town Guilds. Lavish entertainments and musical spectacles were a regular part of Court life, even at international functions such as The Field of the Cloth of Gold in 1520, which must have maintained as many musicians as dignitaries. It was an ideal environment for the development of consorts of instruments. Henry VIII's vast collection included seventy-seven recorders at the time of his death. Each category of instruments was made in several sizes to form consorts. At this time, however, the oboe family in the form of shawms were strictly for the military and town bands. They were a splendid sight and produced a warm, resonant sound. The bass shawm ('pommer' in German) was six feet long and had to be played with the bell resting on the ground.

To discover the various sizes of shawms in the fifteenth century we start with Tinctoris, writing a few years after 1480. He is rather inconclusive. It is well over a century later, in 1618, that we find proof of the complete set in Praetorius. He lists seven from 'klein discant Schalmey' down to 'gross bass pommer', the instruments described above. Not all of these were used at the same time. Often the shawm band would be a mixture of shawms, cornetts and sackbuts. Also, Praetorius is referring to German bands. It is unlikely that so many would have appeared in France or England.

A typical wind orchestra of the period is beautifully illustrated in 'La Procession des Pucelles du Sablon', by the artist Antoine Sallaert, in the Musée de Peinture in Brussels. It is made up of a dulcian, two pommers, a cornett, a shawm and a sackbut. Although shawms and pommers were made to accommodate left- and right-handed players, there is something strangely significant in the fact that Sallaert depicts the dulcian, the pommers and the shawm in the hands of left-handed players. The cornett-player is the only right-handed instrumentalist in the group. This ambidextrous feature of woodwind instruments was sustained right up to the early days of the nineteenth century.

On the larger shawms **(plate 2)** the hole nearest to the bell was too distant for the little finger to reach; it had to be controlled by a lever mounted on a spring, which activated a padded key. The fish-tail shape of the touch-piece was designed to accommodate the little finger of either hand, according to the player's habit. The body of the instrument was in one piece with little or no decoration. Although the outer shape was only slightly curved the inside tube was conical, flaring in a curve at the bell. In order to maintain the simple beauty of the pipe, the key was covered by a perforated wooden barrel (fontanelle) which left only the touch-piece visible. It has also been suggested that the barrel was conceived to protect the keys from damage. The key gave an extra note below the basic octave of intervals derived from the six finger-holes. An extra hole at the bell of the instrument was plugged with wax when tuning demanded it.

The reed was mounted on to a metal staple inserted into the instrument, which also held a wooden, bell-shaped pirouette, against which the lips of the player were pressed. Bate provides good evidence that the player's lips had a little more control over the reed than earlier Eastern players, because the range of the instrument could be 'overblown' above the single octave of notes normally available on instruments which have no thumb-hole. Extra lip-pressure is essential to achieve such an upper range.

For several decades after 1620 Europe was torn apart by the ravages of the Thirty Years War and England was struggling through the events that led to the strife of Cromwell's Commonwealth. We will never know how much fine music was lost or pillaged during these years. So it is even more surprising that the oboe emerged as a prototype in the aftermath of all this.

The story begins in 1651 when Michel Philidor was appointed to the Grand' Ecurie of the French Court as a virtuoso on several wind instruments. (His real name was Danican. Philidor was a name bestowed on him by Louis XIII.) Louis XIV was a boy of thirteen, but was already asserting a love for the arts which eventually won him the epithet of 'Sun King'. Music was uppermost in his pursuits – a fact which marked the destiny of his Court composer, Lully, with more sunlight than any other composer in history. It is certain that Lully consulted Philidor when writing hautbois marches for the Musketeers of Louis XIV. But even more important was the collaboration we may assume between Philidor, a supreme virtuoso, and Hotteterre, the musician who, we think, eventually designed the first oboe. Arriving from Italy where woodwind was in a rather primitive state of development, Lully found the hautbois (shawm) and musette (small bagpipes) in wide use. In the latter years of the 1650s the musical intercourse between these people finally resulted in the birth of the oboe proper. Jean Hotteterre, who was the musette-player at the Court, was principally an instrument-maker. In his workshop the various adaptations and experiments on shawms and musettes eventually brought about an elegant three-jointed oboe which may well have been tried in Lully's ballets before 1660. However, the first recorded adoption was in Cambert's pastoral opera 'Pomone' at the Paris Opera in 1671, a date which truly marks the beginning of orchestral woodwind.

The instrument gained immediate popularity in many countries. By 1695 England had published the first known oboe tutor in 'The Sprightly Companion'. Purcell composed for it as early as 1681 and used it constantly. With the turn of the century the new oboe had won acclaim and wide use throughout Europe and was already inspiring some of the greatest music the Western world has ever known.

By 1715, English town bands had followed the example of the Courts by abandoning the long-used 'waits' in favour of the new hautboy. With this, the shawm family had truly sung its last song.

The two- and three-keyed baroque oboe was used throughout the eighteenth century with very little change. Surprisingly, it was the earlier models from the first half of the century that featured three keys, retaining the fish-tail key for ambidextrous use. After 1750 the two-keyed models required a uniform approach to the hand positions, left above right.

James Talbot provides an invaluable contemporary description of the baroque oboe which lists six finger-holes (three for each hand), the third and fourth featuring double holes to produce the four chromatic notes F, F♯, G, G♯; a pair of small closed keys below D , and a single key below them for C . The bell was long with two tuning-holes. The reed had no pirouette, being left free for the player to manipulate it freely with his lips. The compass embraced two octaves of chromatic intervals: c' to c''', the upper range being produced by biting hard on the reed. He also describes the tenon joints which connect the three sections of the instrument. (See **note on pitches** opposite page 1.)

The modern oboe is able to dispense with the overblowing technique for the second octave of notes by the use of a speaker key. This makes the fingering of the upper octave identical to the lower when the speaker key is operated. No such easy road existed for the baroque oboist. To accommodate the more vagrant tuning of the boxwood instrument, alternative fingerings had to be sought from octave to octave.

Other members of the family

ALTO OBOE (Oboe d'amore/hautbois d'amore)
The oboe was no exception to other instruments in producing several family members of varying sizes and pitches. The oboe d'amore was pitched in A, a minor third lower than the oboe, and was probably used by J. S. Bach as an obbligato instrument because it suited the particular register of the voices it accompanied. The tone-colour was more mellow than the oboe, but more strident than the cor anglais. Although Bach generally used the French name, the instrument is more likely to have been created in Germany in view of the fact that its first recorded use was in German music by G. P. Telemann ('Der Sieg der Schönheit', Hamburg 1722), J. S. Bach (Cantata No. 37, 1725), and in an opera by G. K. Schürmann ('Ludwig der Fromme', 1726).

TENOR OBOE (Oboe da caccia/cor anglais)
The earliest tenor oboes (sometimes mis-named 'alto') were produced at the same time as the parent instrument. Talbot tells us that they were straight, like the oboe. Pitched in F, a fifth lower than the oboe, the bell was flared. They were called 'oboi da caccia' (oboes of the hunt) and were, indeed,

15

used in hunting in the early eighteenth century. When the instrument developed a curve or angle, it was called a cor anglais. Various reasons have been given for these names, such as a mis-spelling of the old French 'cor anglé' (angled horn). No-one knows exactly from where the name was derived, but it has stuck to the instrument we know today ever since it was straightened out again in the nineteenth century.

There is no adequate explanation for the evolution of the bulb-shaped bell on the oboe d'amore and cor anglais. It was an adaptation of the flared bell of the prototype, which may well have been devised for purely practical purposes such as overcoming the difficulty of finding a broad enough section of timber to make the bell in one piece; or simply to minimize the danger of knocking the end of the instrument when used on horseback for military occasions. Whatever the reason, we cannot assume that the bulb-shaped bell has any effect on the tone quality of the instrument. It is simply not true.

Of all the various shapes and sizes of oboes which came out of these first decades of experimentation, the oboe, the oboe d'amore and the cor anglais are the only instruments that have withstood the test of history to appear in the twentieth century as long-standing members of the family. With a few superficial adaptations they constituted the models for which composers wrote from J. S. Bach, in the early 1700s, to early Beethoven, in the 1790s.

Two
Introduction of the Mechanized Oboe

'Can the music that dwells in our souls be other than that which lies enshrined at the heart of nature, like a profound mystery which only a higher intelligence can fathom?' E. T. A. Hoffmann, writing of the new spirit in music at the end of the Napoleonic Wars, heralds the dominant role which Germany was to play throughout the nineteenth century. He was Beethoven's first real commentator, and among his many accomplishments he provided the literary key to the Romantic concept of music as a power to comprehend the world in terms of an aesthetic phenomenon. 'Music and song thus become . . . a hymn of praise to the Creator.' This is the very spirit which inspired the Ninth Symphony. That such an intense pursuit of spiritual values should co-exist with the grime of the Industrial Revolution is an absorbing paradox; yet it is this very duality which created ideal circumstances for the evolution of the mechanized oboe. On the one hand the precision instruments required for making the delicate mechanism were the direct result of machine development, and on the other, the Romantic spirit informed the sound desired from the oboe. Mechanization of wind instruments was never conceived with facility alone as the object. Beauty of tone and articulation were always the prizes sought, and often found.

The box-wood oboe in **plate 3 (b)** is a late model of a classical instrument, probably made during the first decade of the nineteenth century. The bore is identical to all earlier classical models, but the two rounded brass keys are characteristic of the period 1805–40. It was probably made for an elderly oboist who wanted a new instrument in the old style. It is the kind of instrument on which Beethoven's symphonies would have first been heard. By 1830, the young Barret was playing works such as Berlioz' 'Fantastic Symphony' on an ebony Triébert with ten keys and a narrower bore. The difference between the two in tone and articulation is enormous. Anthony Baines provides a table which shows the rapid evolution of the mechanized oboe as played by makers and players such as Barret, Triébert, Boehm and Malsch.

It is at this point that considerations of stylistic adaptation become unnecessary when dealing with matters of interpretation. Since 1830 the fundamental concept of tone production becomes almost identical to our own today. The overblowing technique was superseded by the octave key, and complicated cross-fingering techniques were eliminated by the continually growing number of keys and ring mechanisms. Surprisingly, the man who established the ring and pillar structures which we still use today was not successful in producing a really good oboe. This was Boehm. His oboes were strident and obtrusive in the orchestra.

As in the early days of Hotteterre the principal function of the oboe was in the orchestra. But it must not be assumed that it was unknown as a solo instrument in the nineteenth century. Although it is a common complaint amongst oboists that Brahms never treated them to the luxury of sonatas such as the clarinet works, and that no monumental figures felt moved to write oboe concerti, it must be emphasized that the solo repertoire is amply substantiated by the *petits-maîtres*. When discussing some of the more important of these works it must be kept in mind that the orchestra is where the oboe sustained its essential role through the century.

With the significant exception of Berlioz the mantle of the Romantic movement in music ineluctably falls on Germany. Paradoxically, the evolution of the mechanized oboe, which engendered so much musical thought for Romantic composers, centred on France. For fifty years, while innovation after innovation was made in Paris, Germany desired no developments beyond the model described in Sellner's 'Oboeschule' of 1825. Finally they fell in with the French design during Wagner's later years, although the sound they produced was characteristically more robust and weighty. Austria, on the other hand, sustained the classical model with flared, embossed bell and thick collar, which remains on today's instruments. This Viennese oboe is almost untouched by French influences except in a few details of key-work.

The development of mechanism was a somewhat irregular process. Instrumentalists are notoriously attached to their own instruments, and a change of system which included mechanization may well have been as daring a step for the early nineteenth-century oboist to adopt as the first ride in a mechanical vehicle must have been, when travelling at more than 30 m.p.h. was said to be fatal. The two-keyed instrument of Mozart's orchestra was still used by some players as late as 1820. **Plate 3 (b)** has already been cited as an example of this protracted obsolescence.

By 1825 manufacturers had extended the number of note holes to fifteen, ten of which were controlled by keys which included an octave as 'speaker' key; G♯ key supplementing the double hole of the third finger, right hand; a vent key for the right hand little finger to improve the F♯; a low C♯ key; a closed F key; a closed B♭ key and a closed upper C key. A natural extension of the compass down to B arose with the addition of a long key to cover the tuning hole on the bell. All this meant that the instrument was fully chromatic without need of the complicated fork and cross-fingering which the eighteenth-century instrument required to the degree of entirely different combinations of fingers for relative notes in each octave. The key-work described above went a long way towards resolving many of these problems by the help of the additional holes controlled by the keys.

The French supremacy found its origins in the days of the Revolution. In spite of the rolling heads and the reign of terror, Paris was conscious enough of her cultural heritage to found the great Conservatoire in 1793. One of the most important chairs was for oboe-playing. The first to hold this post were Sallantin and Vogt who mistrusted 'machines' and stuck to their classical two and four-keyed models for life. A

testimony to Vogt's technique can be found in the Otto Langey Tutor where the oboe parts of his concerti are presented
as studies for the modern oboe.

It was Vogt's pupil, Henri Brod (1801-39), who pioneered
some of the first experiments in mechanization. In his
'Method' he claims to have invented the left forefinger plate
which dispensed with the problem of having to half-cover a
hole for C♯. It had the added advantage of improving notes
above c' ". The cor anglais moderne was also pioneered by
him; a straight-bodied instrument with a curved crook. Like
all such innovations these were the common talk of several
craftsmen before their implementation. Brod was certainly a
leader amongst them. The bore of his instruments was very
narrow, and the sound they produced tended to be rather
small and sweet. His death at the early age of thirty-eight
brought mixed comments of praise and disparagement, the
latter from Cherubini. When told, 'Brod est mort, maître',
he replied: 'Qui?' 'Brod.' 'Ah! Petit son (poor tone)!'

His Études and Sonatas demonstrate characteristics
closely akin to Berlioz. Although by no means comparable
as compositions they attest the capabilities of the oboe up to
1840, also providing useful studies for the present day player.

The name which is truly synonymous with the French oboe
is Triébert. Guillaume Triébert began the dynasty by opening
a business in 1810, which flourished till 1876. He was a great
performer and an incomparable craftsman. The family
created six different models, leaving a heritage which still remains the blueprint for all instruments. A complete transformation of the oboe took place under their supervision.
Axles shaped from the wood of the instrument disappeared
in place of pillars screwed directly into it, making the upper
joint completely smooth. By 1840 these pillars carried C, C♯
and D♯ for the right hand little finger; a low B♮ and a dupli-
cate D♯ on a long lever for the left hand little finger; F; F♯
lever was replaced by a 'spectacle' key; a G♯ supplementary
key for the double hole of the third finger, right hand; a half-
hole plate for C♯ and an octave speaker key. This was presented as Système 3.

Système 4 was adopted by Barret, a French expatriate who became solo oboist at Covent Garden in 1829. The addition of a low B♭ key was an important aspect of the instrument he recommended in his 1850 Tutor. Other features included were a ring for the second left hand finger providing a forked C; a key for the C - D trill and touch-levers for the left hand B and D♯. Many oboists today still use a thumb-plate attached to a Conservatoire system oboe. It does not involve too much extra mechanism and has certain advantages of alternative fingering both for intonation inflection and technical facility. For instance the figuration in example 1 is greatly facilitated by the use of a thumb-plate C, dispensing with the right hand forefinger required for the same note on authentic Conservatoire instruments.

Example 1

Mozart *Oboe Quartet, K.370*

Philip Bate explains that the thumb-plate system and open B♭, although usually ascribed to Barret was, in fact, the invention of F. Triébert in 1849, which Barret praises highly in his 1862 Tutor. The system does away with the half-hole characteristic on G, making the upper and lower octaves virtually the same combination of fingers for relative notes. Système 5 included a B♭ key.

Triébert's sixth and last system acknowledged a common dissatisfaction with the thumb-plate and established the use of the right hand forefinger to replace this function for C and B♭. With the addition of an automatic octave key to smooth the change from G - A the basis of the Conservatoire system was laid. After Triébert's death his friend and colleague Lorée took over the firm, continuing the work of experimentation and improvement. With the Système 6 any finger of the right hand could operate the B♭ – C mechanism. George Gillet adopted the system for the Paris Conservatoire in 1882. Since then, this fine instrument has been known as the Conservatoire system. Gillet was also pleased to adopt a later system designed by Lorée which incorporated cover plates on the rings. The system was perfected by his sons and produced in 1906. It is called the 'Gillet model' to distinguish it from the standard Conservatoire instrument.

The subject of mechanization cannot be left without reference to Boehm who invented the system of ring-mechanism used on all woodwind instruments today. The concept of resting a series of rings on rods perched above the finger-holes on pillars screwed into the wood was entirely his. Subsequently the development of his system centred on the flute. Buffet adapted it for the oboe with mixed results. The larger sized holes required for the system became larger and larger under the advice of A. J. Lavigne, a distinguished player who arrived in London in 1841. The sound was very strong and not altogether liked by listeners, so that, even with Lavigne's continued work on developing the system until his death, it was not commonly adopted. The last remnants of the idea can be found on modern oboes made for players who double on the saxophone.

In spite of the standards set by Barret and Lavigne, English oboes were somewhat behind the times throughout the century. In 1840 they only had eight or nine keys. The industry did not flourish so well as in another small country, Belgium, which manufactured some fine models from the Albert family. England simply relied on imported models till very late in the century. Grattan-Cooke played on a simple-system oboe throughout his life with the lowest note sounding C. The following review of Bach's B Minor Mass provides an important comment on this limitation and creates an intriguing speculation on performing conditions in England at this time.

'The chorus is accompanied, we believe, by three obbligati trumpets, the alto tromba extending to E in alt. This part of course Mr. Harper could not play, nor indeed could anybody, with the instrument now in use in our orchestras. The aria "Qui sedes" has an obbligato accompaniment for the tenoroon or oboe d'amore, *an instrument which extended below the Corno Inglese*. This Mr. Grattan Cooke attempted on the common oboe, and, of course, stopped at the very outset of his exertions. The bass solo "Quoniam tu solus", is accompanied by a horn as next to impracticable, and Mr. Denman was furnished with a fagotti-part which appeared greatly incorrect. Of course the selection was slaughtered, with soli-players retiring in dismay, and leaving Mr. Knyvett to play their parts on the organ, which he did most manfully, after the fashion of the men of the last generation, "Solo on the Cornet stop".'

Musical World, 1838

Now, Grattan-Cooke was no fool. An attentive reader will be aware that he was right to attempt the oboe d'amore part on an oboe rather than a cor anglais, because the reviewer is wrong in thinking that the oboe d'amore extends below the cor anglais range. If Cooke had attempted to play on the cor anglais the upper range of the part would have been outside its reasonable capacity. Limited budget performances of the 'St. Matthew Passion' today will rely on the oboes rather than the cor anglais for oboe d'amore solos for the same reason. As for the reference to the tenoroon as a correlative to the oboe d'amore it must be stated that the critic sounds even less accurate than the performance he describes!

The problem was appalling and one wonders how the Bach revival in the nineteenth century could have taken wing under such conditions.

An *Athenaeum* review in 1871 indicates that no radical improvement had been achieved by then:

'It will, of course, be a long time before the intricate music of Bach can be properly and effectively executed; and when a thoroughly efficient ensemble is secured, it will be still doubtful whether the "Passione" according to St. Matthew or St. John can ever be permanently retained in the oratorio repertoire'.

Fortunately, salvation was soon at hand. The Bach Choir was founded in 1876 with a spectacular performance of the B Minor Mass, almost in entirety. Although the absence of instruments relegated the d'amore parts to clarinets on this occasion, it was only two years before the instrument was reintroduced in 1878 by Mallilon of Brussels. In 1885 the

Bach Choir's programme listed the following instrumentalists:

'H. G. Lenon: oboe d'amore

H. Smith: oboe d'amore'

The next decade saw the emergence of J. S. Bach as the timeless genius all oboists would be the first to recognize. Yet no thanks can be offered to the voices that prevailed over fashionable opinion during the century. The outrageous opinions of Dr. Charles Burney, which were so popular, exacerbated the situation:

'If Sebastian Bach and his admirable son Emmanuel, instead of being musical directors in commercial cities, had been fortunately employed to compose for the stage and the public of the great Capitals, such as Naples, Paris, or London, and for performances of the first class, they would doubtless have simplified their style more to the level of their judges; the one would have sacrificed all unmeaning art and contrivance and the other been less fantastical and "recherché", and both, by writing in a style more popular, and generally intelligible and pleasing, would have expended their fame and been indisputably the greatest musicians of the present century'. (*History of Music*, 1776).

Such arrant nonsense gained wide sympathy throughout the classical period and the nineteenth century.

The critic Eduard Hanslick discloses other solutions that were found for the presentation of the St. Matthew Passion in 1862:

'The enjoyment (of the smaller arias) is rendered difficult for the general public, however, by antiquated form and uncommonly paltry instrumentation. The solo voice is frequently accompanied only by oboe and cello . . . each going its own independent way and usually in a strict counterpoint to the voice . . . The smaller aria episodes . . . with two deep oboes (clarinets at this performance), the St. Matthew Passion has in abundance.'

These observations from two great musical capitals like London and Vienna, disclose a curious enigma surrounding the use of the oboe and cor anglais in Bach performances throughout the century. Why should the two cors anglais ('deep oboes') be replaced by clarinets?

In his famous 'Treatise' Berlioz quotes some remarkable examples of their use in Meyerbeer's 'Les Huguenots', and a high-ranging duet in Halévy's 'The Jewess', both composed before 1840. Berlioz' own masterpiece, 'The Fantastic Symphony', gives the instrument solo prominence in the 'Scène aux champs', written in 1829, only two years after Beethoven's death. The answer no doubt lies in the fact that Vienna ignored the French instruments, and the English were slow to adopt them generally, for there is no doubt that the French repertoire maintains very high spots for the cor anglais from the 1820s onwards.

Farcical occasions like the 1838 performance of the B Minor Mass were more common in the early years of the century than may be imagined. Witness J. F. Reichardt attending a benefit concert for Beethoven on 22 December 1808. The concert included first performances of the Sixth Symphony; 'Ah, Perfido' Op. 65; the Gloria and Sanctus from the Mass in C; the Fourth Piano Concerto (played by Beethoven); the Fifth Symphony, and the Choral Fantasy. This took four hours and was performed in freezing cold conditions. 'Poor Beethoven', writes Reichardt, 'who had from this concert his first and only ready profit of the whole year, found considerable hostility and only feeble support in the arrangements and performance. The singers and orchestra were made up of very heterogeneous elements, and it had not even been possible to arrange one full rehearsal of all the pieces on the programme, every one of which was filled with the greatest difficulties.'

These 'difficulties' are perhaps the most significant feature in all Beethoven's music, the very aspect indeed that distinguishes him from classical and truly romantic epithets. Like Bach, he was not a child of his time, and may well have been the first composer in history to compose music that was consistently and unremittingly difficult to learn. His life was hinged on such performances as those which Reichardt describes. Although recognized as the great musical force which history has acknowledged, the isolation he suffered in Vienna seems quite pathetic when we hear him in 1822 explaining to a Leipzig editor: 'You will hear nothing of me here. What should you hear? Fidelio? They cannot give it, nor do they want to give it. The symphonies? They have no time for them. My concertos? Everyone grinds out only the stuff he himself has made. The solo pieces? They went out of fashion long ago, and here fashion is everything'. It is the common tale of many great artists in history. Nevertheless, it is a fact that Beethoven continually demanded substance from his instruments that was totally unprecedented, requiring from his players the will to extend their expressive and technical range of performance. The oboe was no exception. It must be remembered that during the period Beethoven was composing his Symphonies Nos. 1–8, the classical oboe was in an obsolescent state, while the mechanized instrument was taking very tentative steps of evolution towards the oboe for which Berlioz and Wagner composed.

The Bass Oboe and Heckelphone

Experimental instruments sounding an octave lower than the oboe proper were produced as early as 1825 by Triébert and Brod. In 1889 Lorée designed the bass oboe we use today, with a compass reaching down to B.

Heckel (the bassoon manufacturer) produced another model in 1904 which descended even farther, down to A.

There is very little distinction between the sounds of the bass oboe and the heckelphone. Parts written for an oboe in this register can be played on either instrument with equal quality. Holst used its deep, rich and reedy voice in 'Saturn' (from 'The Planets' Suite) to evoke all the darkness of a relentless dirge. Strauss used it in 'Salome' and 'Elektra' with more exotic taste. Its rare use by modern composers is no criterion of its magic effect. **(Plate 4 (b).)**

Since 1880 the prime characteristics of the oboe have not changed. Additional keys and vents have been added from time to time, but these can only be considered as improvements on an established format, rather than revolutionary changes comparable with the early Triébert instruments. My own Lorée serves me as well today as it did in 1907, when I first played it.

In some ways we are in danger of allowing technology to

become an end in itself, for we are gradually developing mechanical improvements at the expense of the delicacy so lovingly wrought by the Triéberts and the Lorées. Some modern instruments are so overweighted with mechanism and wood that I would find it extremely difficult to endure a recital with one, no matter how cleanly the keys may operate.

The oboe is a lady. If we lose her feminine qualities we neutralize the sound which thousands of years of history have sought to sustain and beautify. Oboists, like all musicians, have a Muse to protect. Let us see Truth in Beauty and guard our musical sensibilities with this aim.

Part Two

The Reed and the Oboist

Three
The Reed

The oboe is one of the most idiosyncratic of all instruments. No two players will produce an identical tone quality, even if playing on the same instrument and the same reed. The individual personality of an oboist is reflected in the performance to an extreme degree. In spite of this, the principles underlying reed-making* and the technique of playing are very broadly based. In this section I shall examine the procedures that have proved successful for me. Beyond that, I claim no authority for foolproof methods. So much depends on the self-awareness of the player in adapting these fundamentals to his own physiognomy and artistic taste.

A clear concept of tone quality is of paramount importance at every stage in the oboist's development. Without this he/she is working blindfolded. The quality of the instrument asserts considerable influence on the concept, but not so much as the reed. Therefore, it is reed-making and scraping which fulfils the primary functions of tone-quality no matter what make of instrument is chosen. In discussing the principles of technique involved in this process I must emphasize that the principles themselves are of no value unless supported by a concept of the sound desired. Although this is personal to a great extent, the following points are important in reaching a conclusion:

1 *Tone.* It must be possible to achieve extremes of dynamic range while sustaining a good tone quality.

2 *Tongue.* The reed must be hard enough to give substance

---

*All serious oboists make their own reeds; the generally interested reader may care to skip this chapter.

to the tone, but soft enough to retain freedom to tongue easily and quickly.

3 *Projection.* This is always important whether playing soft or loud passages.

4 *Breath Control.* The reed must be responsive enough to meet the constant air-pressure controlled by the diaphragm.

5 *Embouchure.* To take all these points into account, all conditions must make it possible to sustain a relaxed embouchure. No performer can learn the endurance demanded of the Strauss Concerto with tight or stiff lips.

Reed-making equipment

With these points in mind let us consider the reed. **Plate 5** shows the tools required for reed-making. A list of dealers and manufacturers is shown in Appendix 1.

The Knife. At least two knives are essential; an extra one for rough scraping is also advisable. The steel plaque used to secure the cane in the scraping process blunts the knife very quickly, therefore a good quality knife should be kept for finishing off. A blunt knife used in the final stage when the tip of the reed is very thin may tear the fibres and ruin the reed. Scraping knives are made of very hard, tempered steel. Flexibility in a blade is by no means a good qualification. The blade is 4–5in long, ⅛in thick, and ½in deep. There are two kinds in common use: a chisel shape with one side flat, the other chamfered for scraping to an angle of 45 degrees (**fig. 1**). The other kind is a hollow-ground blade with the same basic proportions, but equally honed on both sides from the thick to the scraping edge. Like an open razor the shape of the scraping edge is always maintained if both edges are pressed hard against the stone when sharpening (**fig. 2**).

The other essential kind is the *trimming knife* used for cutting off the tips of reeds. This must be very sharp as well, but, unlike the scraping knife, it needs a cutting edge ground equally on both sides of the blade.

Knives with large handles are preferable, to avoid cramp when using for long periods.

PLATE ONE *Above* A double-aulos player. Fresco from the Tomb of the Leopards, Tarquinia. B.C. 480–470.
Left An aulos player softening the reed of his instrument.

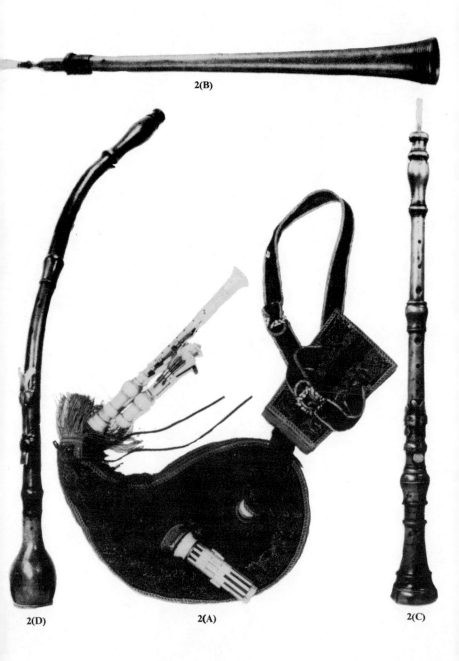

PLATE TWO *Below* Shawm; German, late 16th century. *Bottom, left to right* Curved cor anglais; Italian, late 18th century. Musette, showing bellows. Oboe; Stanesby, London, early 18th century.

2(B)

2(D)   2(A)   2(C)

PLATE THREE *From left to right* Oboe; W. Milhouse, c 1785.
Classical oboe; Noblet fréres, c 1800. Lorée oboe, 1907; Lorée oboe,
1975. Oboe d'amore; Louis, 1925. Cor anglais; Rigoutat, 1950.

PLATE FOUR *From left to right* Tenor oboe; M. Lot, c 1775. Bass (baritone) oboe; Triébert, 1825. Cor anglais; C. Golde, 1840 (curved). Oboe, Tabard, c 1830.

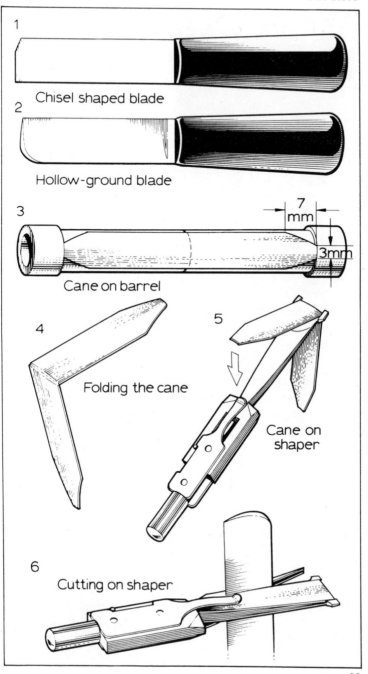

1 Chisel shaped blade

2 Hollow-ground blade

3 7 mm 3mm Cane on barrel

4 Folding the cane

5 Cane on shaper

6 Cutting on shaper

Sharpening Stone. It is vital to choose a stone of adequate proportions to ensure that all the blade is kept in contact with the stone while sharpening. This is necessary in order to maintain an even edge on the knife. The most suitable stone is a carborundum type; 8in × 2in × ¾in. A 'fine' grade will prevent heavy wear on the knife and produce the finest edge on the blade. The only use for a coarse-grade stone is for honing-down a damaged or over-blunt blade. To prevent clogging in the pores of the stone it should be oiled before use. Fine key oil or sewing-machine oil is best. Saliva is even cheaper!

There are several ways to sharpen the knives. The one I prefer is as follows. The scraping knife needs a slightly curved or rough edge. For the chisel-shaped blade it is a straightforward task. Alternate the strokes diagonally across the stone pushing away from the body towards the cutting edge, then draw it back in a circular motion; first, the straight back of the blade, then the 45 degree edge. Always finish with the latter to achieve the slight curve or roughness required to grip the cane fibres. The same kind of stroke is suitable for the hollow-ground blade as well, again finishing with the strokes pushing away from the body. The general principle underlying this procedure shows that whether the oboist is left-handed or right-handed the final strokes should curve the edge slightly in the same direction in which the scraping strokes are made.

Before using the knife to scrape the reed great care should be taken to ensure that all the oil is wiped from the blade and fingers.

The Cutting Block. A circular wooden block with a slightly curved surface on the cutting side, used for cutting the tip of the reed. They come in various sizes.

The Scraping Tongue (or **Plaque**). A flat oval plate of steel. The standard size is 1½in × ½in. Some players prefer a narrower plate to prevent the knife from coming into contact at the edges. There is a danger that this will not provide sufficient support for the reed when the lay (see p. 44) is being scraped. These plaques are often made of African blackwood. An added danger here is that the surface will quickly become gouged with knife strokes and infiltrate fibres into the cane of the reed. The present writer prefers the traditional steel plaque described above.

The Mandrel. This is a steel rod mounted in a handle. The end is elliptical, gradually becoming circular to fit the shape of the staple tube for which it is designed. It has several functions: in the tying-on process it prevents the staple from collapsing under the pressure of the binding; it helps the maker to hold the reed firmly while tying-on; when pushed hard into the staple it can correct any mis-shaping the tube may have suffered. For this last purpose it is wise to use a mandrel made by the same manufacturer as the staples you use. Both items come in many different sizes and shapes; but individual manufacturers make one to fit the other. Like all other aspects of good oboe technique, consistency is the cardinal rule once a process has been established.

Staples are probably the most important item as the sound-source end of the vibrating column. They should be 47mm long and conical. Although they are made of brass, silver, copper and alloys, like most professional reed-makers I prefer brass for the clear resonance its surface provides. Copper oxidizes and other softer metals fail to stimulate the harmonic resonances which brass induces. It is imperative that the cork surrounding the base of the tube is not broken or cracked. Moisture easily collects in such crevices.

Cane. Gouged cane can be purchased at all manufacturers and firms listed in Appendix 1. The gouging process (discussed on pp. 37–8) may be left to a professional reed-maker without problems. But it is essential for the player to take over at the shaping stage. Nowhere else is our rule for consistency more important than in the shaping of the cane. The thickness of the cane is dictated in the gouging process and individual requirements can be met with the following scale in mind:

Soft reeds (suitable for a beginner) 20 thousandths of an inch.

Medium-soft (suitable for high-ranging contemporary music demanding a wide range of variable articulations) 21 thousandths.

Medium (suitable for general orchestral playing) 22 thousandths.

The diameter of the gouge is important for obtaining the required aperture and applies to all thicknesses:

11½mm: close
11mm: fairly close
10½mm: medium

Ruler. This should show millimetres and inches, being especially important for checking the measurement of the finished reed.

Barrel (or **Easel**). A circular piece of metal or wood with a mark around the centre to gauge the mark across the bending point of the cane. The inside measurement is 77mm. The ends of the reed should be trimmed on this implement.

Binding Thread is a fairly standard tying-on thread obtainable at all dealers listed in Appendix 1. Nylon thread is used by some makers, but this necessitates the extra chore of waxing.

Goldbeater's Skin. A very thin, transparent animal skin used for wrapping around the base of the tied-on cane to prevent air leaking between the blades. It has the unusual quality of being airtight and waterproof; also, it is self-adhesive and does not interfere with the free vibration of the blades.

Pliers and **Scissors** are useful for general adjustments and cutting. Pliers should be small with pointed jaws. They are used for adjusting the aperture of a badly shaped staple and gripping the end of an unscrewed rod when releasing keys for oiling and repair. Scissors should be available for cutting thread after tying on.

Shaper. A small adjustable metal blade for moulding the shape of the cane.

Gouging

'The reed of the oboe is what the larynx is to the human voice'. The analogy I quote from my biography sums up the most essential aspect of my concept of the oboe. It has been attested by singers who have approached me for help over breath-control problems. Above all, the oboe must sing. It can only do this if the reed permits. A singer with a cold is like an oboist with a poor reed. The oboist is luckier, however, if he has taken the trouble and time to master the art of reed-making; for he need never be without the means to replace a malfunctioning reed.

The first stage of this art is gouging.

In its basic condition the cane begins as a tube. The finest quality is an ivory colour and should be selected on this criterion. Variable diameters are available, and the cane measure **(plate 6)** provides a gauge for six sizes. A good average is $10\frac{1}{2}$–11mm. The surface of the cane must be absolutely smooth, without a trace of ribs.

While the cane is dry a splitting tool is used to divide the tube into three equal strips, which are fairly thick. **(Plate 6.)**

Choose the best section of the cane approximate to the length of the pre-gouging bed on the gouging machine **(plate 7 (a))**. The selected section of the tube must be as straight as possible to achieve a secure position in the pre-gouging bed. Any misalignment can cause the cane to jump when the gouging blade is operated. Pare the edges to prevent splitting, then use the guillotine **(plate 6)** to chop the correct length. Place the strip in the pre-gouging bed **(plate 7)** and plane across several times with a firm stroke to form the sides of the shape before gouging.

At this point the cane must be soaked for four to five

hours, then placed in the gouging bed. Pull down the blade assembly **(plate 7 (a))** and plane with a firm hand-pressure several times until no more shavings appear **(plate 8 (a)).**

A micrometer **(plate 9 (a))** with a ball-and-anvil should then be used to check the thickness of the gouge, which is dictated by the setting of the gouging machine. Further checks are useful with the help of a radius gauge to ensure that no malformation has occurred during the gouging process.

Shaping

This is the most idiosyncratic stage of reed-making. Experimentation and deductions from various proportions are ultimately the only basis for satisfaction. Each experienced oboist will have a different story to tell and each one may be completely justified if the performance is as confident as the theory. The fact remains, however, that trial and error is the only sure road to finding proportions which are agreeable to the individual constitution of the player and his/her concept of sound. The best foundation for beginning the quest is to use a shape (see **plate 6)** measuring 7mm at the widest point of the reed shaper. This is fairly broad but provides a wide aperture which can be made smaller by chamfering with a sandpaper board when the reed is tied on. The broadest shape provides the widest aperture. Another factor that dictates the width of the aperture is the diameter of the cane in its pre-gouged condition (see pp. 36–7). The shaper is made of hard steel in the shape of the reed blades. The related proportions of the throat (lower, narrow end) and the tip of the shape are manufactured in many different measurements, a fact which emphasizes the necessity to experiment with various tools before choosing. German and Italian shapes generally have a rather narrow base which, of course, is ideal for the proportions of German and Italian staples. My own experience with a French instrument naturally encourages me to recommend a shape appropriate to French staples, which tend to be larger in bore. For this reason a less shallow taper towards the base will suit French requirements more satisfactorily. If these proportions are not observed the tying-on will be affected badly, and leaky, maladjusted blades will result.

The writer claims no distinction in the following recommendations for shaping and tying-on. It is simply one method among many which has been proved successful.

1. Soak the gouged cane in tepid water from 50 minutes to an hour. A sure sign that the cane is soaked sufficiently for pliable manipulation can be seen when it sinks. Wiping off the bubbles that sometimes appear on the cane when first submerged can provide an added precaution against over-soaking; cane can be permanently spoiled if it becomes waterlogged.

2. Place the soaked cane on the barrel and taper both sides at each end in the shape of a triangle, 7mm at the sides and 3mm across the base (fig. 3). This should leave the bark unscraped in the centre, about the width of the staple at the point where the end of the reed is placed before tying on, approximately 3mm wide. Eventually this will be tapered, but it is wise to leave it at this stage in order to avoid splitting when the cane is secured to the shape. Cut off the tapered triangles with the cutting knife.

   The line around the centre of the barrel (plate 5) marks the point where the knife should be rolled lightly across the bark three or four times, sufficiently to mark the cane for a clean bend. Avoid too deep a cut. If the cane breaks before tying on is completed, it is useless.

3. Remove the cane from the barrel and fold it at the centre (fig. 4).

4. Place the folded cane on the shape blade (fig. 5). If it is too broad to fit easily between the blade torrets, trim the area around the fold. It is very important to ensure that the grain of the cane is in perfect line with the steel blade. Tighten the cane holders to secure both blades. Then shape the cane by drawing a knife down the sides, taking care to keep the knife-blade at a 90 degree angle to the flat blade of the shape (fig. 6). Any unevenness at this stage will create leaks between the blades of the completed reed. It is

necessary to bring the blade to the bottom of the shape to meet the steel shoulder at the base. Inevitably this knife will develop a rather rough edge.

5. Remove the shaped cane from the shaper, then taper the remaining bark at the end of each blade. It is safest to put the cane on the barrel for this operation. If this part of the bark is left on there will be a lump in the binding which can cause leaks and mis-shaping.

Binding

If enough time has elapsed to allow the cane to dry out after shaping, be sure to soak it again before binding. Here again, several methods can be recommended:

Cut about one yard of binding from the spool. Tie one end to a strong support such as a door-knob (locked for safety!) or a hook. To increase the resistance to snapping at this anchor point it is best to fold four or five inches of the securing end to make the knot a double thickness. Take the loose end and form a loop about four inches from the tied knot by passing the binding over from right to left, then upwards through the resulting loop (**fig. 7**). Leaving a small loop about $\frac{1}{2}$in in diameter, take the staple and insert the mandrel. Some players measure the length of cane to be placed over the tube of the staple by marking 27mm from the tip. Others recommend placing the ends of the cane 7 or 8mm over the tube or about half-way between the cork and the tip (**fig. 8**). Either way, it must be kept in mind that if the cane is placed too far down the tube the fulcrum of the cane (or balance point of pressure) will close, diminishing the aperture. Too wide an aperture will result if the cane is not placed far enough over the tube, and the reed will leak at the sides. Holding the blades against the tube with finger and thumb of one hand, use the other for manipulating them to a straight and central position, ensuring an even space between the blades on both sides. Then insert the cane into the loop of the binding, again securing the blades with one hand. Take the loose end of the binding with the other hand and pull the loop tight around the cane very near to the top of the staple

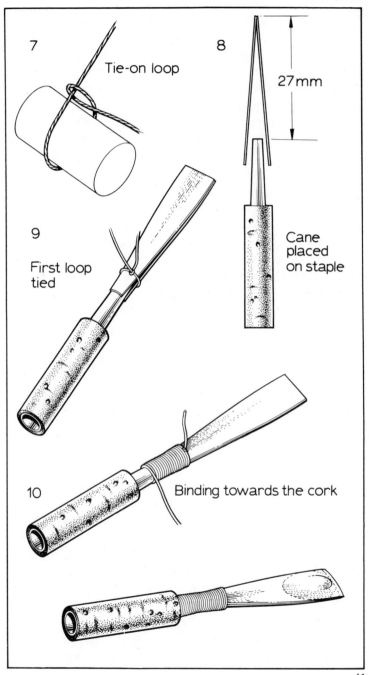

7 Tie-on loop

8 27mm

Cane placed on staple

9 First loop tied

10 Binding towards the cork

(fig. 9). Some players prefer to begin binding without a loop, especially if a preference is made for leaving the binding connected to the spool – a good way to avoid cutting fingers. However, the value of the loop lies in the secure knot which sustains the first binding loop around the cane and staple, providing an extra opportunity for adjusting any malformation resulting from the first strain put upon the cane.

Bind towards the tip of the reed making sure that both sides of the cane close together equally around the neck of the staple. If the measurements recommended have been adopted and each loop of the binding is pulled firmly, the gaps should close equally at the neck end of the staple. Binding beyond the top of the staple will create many problems in playing.

At this point begin to bind across the existing loops towards the staple cork **(fig. 10).** A single loop may be sufficient before reaching the other secured end of the binding. Loops at this point should be made over the secured end of the binding while sustaining firm tension on both ends. Continue binding almost to the cork, then secure with two knotted loops around the tied end and cut free. Nail varnish or a similar cement substance painted over the knot and binding will help to secure it.

Scraping

Use the 'rough-scraping' knife to begin. Take a few strokes from below the tip (about 5mm) to take off the heavy bark at the join, before cutting off the tip.

Then insert the tongue between the tips of the two blades and begin to scrape. Take care to insert the tongue far enough between the blades to make it secure, while taking equal precaution against forcing and splitting. The knife must be sharp at all times so that the stroke does not at any time dig into the cane. The diagram in **fig. 11** shows the areas which the scrape aims to design. Each stroke must be carefully considered.

The general shape is made by beginning with strokes close to the tip and gradually making each one longer, but always continuing over the tip. Repeated several times the slope will

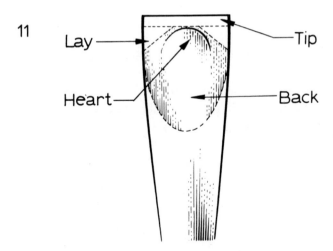

11 Lay — Tip

Heart — Back

develop evenly. The reed and mandrel should rest across the palm of the hand diagonally. The knife should be held with the thumb resting on the back of the blade to control the swing of the knife. It is very important to maintain a relaxed grip to ensure that the stroke is not harsh. The left (or supporting) hand should remain immobile with the thumb resting across the back of the blade as a pivot, while the right (or knife-) hand performs the rocking motion of the scrape. Be careful to incline the knife blade towards the tip. In order to prevent a hump at the tip, each stroke should be diagonal, alternating right and left to achieve an equally balanced shape. **(Plate 8 (b).)**

There are three basic forms for the shape of the scrape: a 'U', a 'V' and a 'W'. The latter is a long scrape which leaves a strong line of bark along the centre of the blades with fairly exaggerated Vs on either side. It is advocated by Janet Craxton and has the virtue of being fairly easy to play for long periods while sustaining a firm quality of sound. The V shape is used by many European and American players. This again has the virtue of easy response, but it is easy to scrape too much from the shoulder. Without shoulder support and with so little bark the reed can easily collapse.

My own preference is for the U shape advocated by a maker who possessed qualities of genius, T. Brearley of Liverpool, who died in 1952. No-one has surpassed the consistency of quality which his green fingers could mould from a piece of cane.

Once the basic shape is formed the final shaping with the elements indicated in **fig. 11** should be done over a period of a few days allowing the fibres to settle a little after each scraping. It is best to have several reeds constantly ready at this stage. A reed will change its character from day to day during the scraping process and it is all too easy to take off too much wood. The finishing knife needs to be sharpened often to avoid tearing the cane at the tip. During this period the tip and the lay need gradual thinning with very light strokes of the knife. However, strokes should always be drawn fairly quickly. If they are sluggish, unevenness of pressure can cause humps and poor response. Hold the reed against the light – preferably sunlight – to check the development of the shape. Uniformity of both blades is a prime essential. These aspects can be checked as follows:

1. Wet the tip of the reed with the tongue and hold the blades against the light in a convenient position to look along them. If one blade is thicker than the other the light will reflect a wall along the edge of the tip.

2. The gradation of the lay towards the top of the shoulder should be an even slope. Look along the edge of the reed to check that the shoulder begins at the same point on both blades. The tip and the lay should eventually form the shape of a half-moon.

3. Most important: the length of scrape must be the same on both blades. If the pivot position of the left-hand thumb (for a right-handed person) is constant throughout the scraping process, the depth of the blade should dictate this fairly accurately. 7–9mm is an average length for this scrape.

When the reed is approaching completion in the shape described, 'croaking' should be possible. Blow the reed without the instrument and a note approximately B should be heard. If this croak is not easily obtainable a very gentle scrape over the length of the blades will help.

Check the pitch by playing the reed in the instrument against an A440 tuning-fork. An average length for the whole reed is 72mm. For a beginner a shorter length of cane and scrape provides an easier response; 70mm for the reed and 6mm for the scrape.

Throughout the scraping process we can improve on Aristotle's recommendation to 'moisten with saliva'. It is much better to soak it in water for 10–15 minutes before scraping or playing on a new reed. Saliva creates a crusty coating on the cane which ultimately destroys its vibrating quality. Therefore, as often as possible use water for soaking.

With a little water goldbeater's skin can be wound around the base of the cane and part of the binding as a precaution against minute leaks.

The length of the scrape is an important factor in determining the pitch at which the instrument will play. Adjustments can be made if this is not correct. For a reed that plays sharp, lengthen the back of the scrape, always directing the knife diagonally to avoid digging and to sustain the substantial amount of wood in the heart. A general approach towards the manner of stroke used with the knife should include an awareness of the behaviour of cane fibres. It is not simply the two blades that vibrate against each other but the individual fibres vibrating together within a single blade. If these fibres are frayed by a rough knife or too much pressure the potential of the reed is immediately diminished. For this reason it is important to avoid dragging the knife back over the cane after a forward stroke has been made.

There follows a brief list of common faults and ways of correcting them:

1. **Too Hard.** What qualifies for this category varies considerably from player to player. It is damaging for a beginner to play on any but a soft, easy-speaking reed, and discouraging for a more mature player to persist with a hard reed, in the fond belief that hardness is essential to good quality. All

considerations for the type of resistance in relation to sound quality rest on fluency and freedom from any kind of tension or strong pressure. While preserving the substance of the heart, the reed requires a general scrape until it is possible to play without tenseness or force. In thinning the lay in these circumstances it is useful to have a slight curve at the end of the knife-blade. Many manufacturers produce knives of this sort, and save many a heart being torn out of a reed by an unintended stroke from a blade concentrating on the lay.

Another common reason for hardness is the condition of too wide an aperture. The aperture of the reed is the most important constant of all. The directions already given to produce correct proportions may not always provide an adequate result if the cane has been bought already gouged. Without precision instruments the proportions cannot be properly checked. Any miscalculation resulting from this can affect the size of the aperture. Take a little from the heart and the back of the scrape to weaken the spring in the reed. If this does not work it is better to dispose of it. Wiring with thin wire (about the thickness of 15amp fuse wire) and closing the wound disc with pliers can provide rescue, but this tends to diminish control of the reed by stifling the natural vibration of the cane.

2. **Too Soft:** There are several possible reasons for this condition. If the cane has been tied too low on the staple, the aperture will undoubtedly be too closed, making the pitch too high and the response very weak. There is only one thing to do with such a reed: untie it and start again. Some players recommend a pinch with pliers at the neck of the staple, or turning the reed sideways to pinch the staple halfway between the neck and the cork. By altering the position of the fulcrum in this way the aperture of the reed will widen. However, this can affect the general intonation of the instrument and is not recommended by the present writer. The same consequence can occur when pitch adjustment is made by filing down or cutting off a portion from the base of the staple. Any attempt

to alter the length or proportions of a staple will certainly affect the general intonation adversely.

If the aperture is reasonably springy and appears to be correct, but adequate resistance is lacking, it is likely that too much cane has been taken from the heart. All things are relative in the proportions of the cane, so it is worth taking off a small portion from the tip. This results in the tip being slightly thicker than before and consequently stronger in relation to the heart. With very minute strokes re-scrape the lay to re-form the tip. This will provide more body. Intonation will not be affected by this procedure because lengthening the lay has the effect of lowering the pitch, and with care will compensate for the shorter length of cane resulting from the cut tip.

Faulty proportions in cane that is gouged by a manufacturer may cause a closed aperture. It is likely that wiring may be the only salvation possible. Before resorting to this procedure there is one more scraping process to try. Form a small groove very close to the tip taking care not to allow the knife to travel across the tip itself. Making the area immediately behind it thinner than the tip itself can induce more spring in the blades, and open the aperture a little. However, it is better not to waste time if the initial efforts fail at this stage. A well-proportioned reed made correctly at all stages is a much safer and satisfactory instrument to play.

A faulty reed may easily be wrongly diagnosed as a fault in the instrument. To set a rule on this can save much heartache. When faults appear try the instrument with several different reeds before taking out the screwdriver. Significant among these conditions is an inability for the upper range above c''' to speak. This could simply mean that the scrape is too long. Cut off the tip of the reed to change the relationship of thickness between heart and back. Other extremes of this condition relate to the length of the scrape. If the upper notes are sharp, the scrape is too short; if the lower notes are flat the scrape is too long. Adjustments to the reed already prescribed can correct these pitch errors. Special care must always be taken to keep the tip very short indeed. A long tip and lay will produce harshness, flatness and possibly a 'quacky' tone. The opposite is the case when too much wood is left at the back of the scrape. Difficulty with lower notes and a certain stuffiness of tone are the usual characteristics of this condition. A light scrape from the back towards the heart will ease the situation and mellow the sound considerably. Diagonal scrapes between the heart and the tip will help to avoid bumps and walls of cane between each area.

Good tone quality and correct proportions for a good reed go hand in hand with the embouchure. No concept can be fulfilled if this relationship is ignored. Embouchure is a very personal matter. When considering general principles it is not enough to 'do as the tutor-book advises'. Many experiments are required with harder or softer reeds, and no amount of instruction can assist if the reed is wrong for the individual formation of the embouchure. It is sometimes better to forget the word in the early stages of playing. Simply consider the position of the reed on the lower lip. Like reed-shapers, lips come in various sizes; therefore, consider that the tip of the reed needs to remain in contact with the lower lip when set in vibration. A player who takes too much reed in the mouth may well be allowing the tip to vibrate without control inside. If the tip is not in contact with the bottom lip, little control of nuance, attack and dynamics can be attained, even if the fundamental sound is satisfactory.

A pliable embouchure can be cultivated only if the reed avoids the condition of being over-resistant. A stiff embouchure is the result of a stiff reed. Ideally one needs to think in terms of withdrawing the tip to play nearer the sensitive ends of the two blades so that the tongue and lip can remain free from tenseness. To attain this condition it is essential to use a reed which vibrates easily. Good tone quality may best be sustained with a relaxed embouchure.

Cor Anglais Reeds

Points of special consideration relating to cor anglais reeds must include the extra equipment required:

1. A cor anglais barrel (easel)
2. A shaper blade
3. Cor anglais staples.

The gouging process should produce the proportions of the cane strip at 95mm × 8.5 (or 9) mm. The cutting process is exactly the same for both instruments. The shape also follows the oboe process. It is the staple that marks the main difference, being a simple conical metal tube that slips over the crook. More than any other factor it is essential to have a staple that fits the bore of the crook evenly. Staples vary considerably. One that is wrongly proportioned in relation to the bore of the crook will leak and make it impossible to play. Again, the manufacturer of the staple must be the same as for the crook.

Wiring is imperative for a cor anglais reed because the broader and long strip cannot provide sufficient control over the aperture. The wire is turned twice below the scrape and twisted. Pliers are used to squeeze the wire in opening and closing the aperture to a suitable degree. Goldbeater's skin is also an imperative to cover the area around the wire and part of the binding, safeguarding against leaks, and protecting the lips in case of contact with the wire.

The crook has far more effect on the quality of intonation than the reed. A German crook on a French-bored instrument is grievous for intonation. Proportions vary enormously between one manufacturer and another. Again, the rule is that the same maker must be responsible for the crook, the instrument and the staple. If a player is using a second-hand instrument with an unsympathetic crook, an earnest quest for the right crook can save many a tear!

Oboe d'Amore Reeds

Specifications are similar to the cor anglais. The proportions of the finished reed are 7mm × 55mm. The staple is considerably smaller but the reed still requires wiring. Cautionary advice about appropriate staples and crooks in relation to the make of instrument are equally applicable.

Four

General Aspects of Modern Techniques

The following summary of first principles relates to aspects of technique which need constant attention and re-thinking again and again throughout a performer's life. It is hoped that readers will not share my own experience in having to reform their technique as the result of a shattered jaw; but this incident is perhaps an extreme example of the physical changes one can go through in life either by the normal process of ageing, by dental adjustments or (as in my case) as a result of accident. Whatever the case, adjustment to physical changes is an important part of sustaining a vital and assertive approach to playing.

The recent proliferation of woodwind playing in schools has led more and more young people into oboe playing. As a result, manufacturers have to work under great pressure to keep up with rising demands for new orders. With waiting lists up to three years the beginner will have little chance of finding a professional model which could be considered satisfactory for orchestral playing. For a musical pupil so much importance is attached to the quality of the instrument chosen that few compromises can be made. Good student models have proved of great value in bridging the gap until a professional model can be purchased. Appendix 1 contains a list of manufacturers who supply reliable models.

Maintenance

Paradoxically it is the professional instruments, which have much more key-work and (usually) narrower bores, that create most difficulties in their first months of work. Many sad stories have come my way of new instruments that develop cracks in the first few months of life, damaged to the point of having to be replaced. There are several possible reasons for this sad situation. The African blackwood, from which most oboes are made today, is extremely hard. Occasionally some minor knots may be present in the wood. There is no reason why they should be harmful unless they appear in a region in line with the pillars or finger-holes. The leverage on springs and the stresses this creates can encourage the development of a crack or a split at the weakest side of the bore where the pillars rest or finger-holes are set. The upper joint, being a narrower bore than the middle joint, with a concentration of small holes towards the top, is more likely to be prone to cracks.

Climatic conditions can also present dangers. Visiting Iceland, I once heard tales from English oboists who had to face sudden changes of temperature on their appointments to the Reykjavik Orchestra. Splits galore!

It need not happen.

My own instrument, made in 1907, has travelled with me all over the world and in all sorts of climatic conditions. But I have always taken great care to prepare it for countries of extreme temperatures. Oil is the answer. It is the life-pulse of any machine and oboes are no exception. The type of thin linseed oil recommended by manufacturers is best.

This is very thin and easily absorbed. Thick oil will remain on the surface and eventually clog the bore by attracting dirt. To avoid spoiling pads it is best to remove the keywork. Soak a pheasant feather (cured at your butcher's) and lightly pass it through the bore of the instrument. While the springs are exposed take the opportunity to clean and oil them a little before replacing the mechanism on newly oiled screws and rods. This should be done every two to three years; minor oiling, once every six months or so. Having stated this, a warning must follow. Don't overdo it! Too much oiling and too often will certainly have the opposite effect intended on the mechanism.

A new instrument should not be played too often for the first six months of its life. The wood needs to settle. An hour a day at first is all the upper joint can take until the instrument has adjusted to expanding and contracting in varying temperatures.

During my honeymoon in Austria, the conductor Furt-wängler asked my wife, 'Is your husband still playing the oboe?' He was most surprised when he learnt that I was indeed. 'Oh, most of my players give up when they're 35 to 40,' he replied, 'the strain is too much.'

This tells us a great deal about the strain exerted on most players earlier in this century, who used hard reeds to establish a good tone. Generally, the French and English sound was more wooden than we hear today, and many oboists had shorter careers as a consequence of over-exertion while playing. Charles Reynolds, my own teacher, often sent Brearley to deputize for him. His mastery of reed-making has already been praised, and I consider myself very lucky to have learned to play on the softer, more lucidly expressive reeds he designed for me. I have used the same kind of reed and scrape ever since. Control of articulation and dynamics is more easily attainable on this kind of pliable reed. Reynolds used a handkerchief draped below the music desk of his stand to dampen the sound in the long pianissimo sections of Wagner's operas. 'Muting' in this way is a valid form of 'sotto voce' playing. Other players use a wad of cotton wool to put in the bell of the instrument. This can have unintended amusing consequences, but it is an effective form of damping if rests permit. Intonation needs to be carefully adjusted, especially on e'. Anything below d' is impossible, of course. Ideally, it is better to adjust the reed than to use a mute. (See **pitch chart** opposite page 1.)

Considering the close correlation of all facets of oboe technique, it must be stressed that if one aspect is unsatisfactory the whole presentation will suffer profoundly. If the reed is too hard, breathing suffers and throat muscles become strained into action. This is poor for health as well as for music. If the diaphragm does not supply sufficient support for the breath, even on a soft reed, the sound will be weak and lack projection. If the embouchure is too tight around the reed, tonguing will be laboured and finger facility and co-ordination very sluggish. All aspects of controlled playing must be free from tension.

The Teacher

The first lesson a pupil receives may well be the most important of all. Every aspect of technical development is founded here. Therefore, a concept of the mature player must inform every comment the teacher makes. For instance, breath-control is a complicated matter to explain to a young pupil. Nevertheless, a simple way of expressing the fundamental matter of breathing has to be found, so that the conditions for developing correct habits of control may be laid. It takes much longer to *un*learn a bad habit than it does to learn a good one. This correlation of fundamentals for a beginner, along with the concept of the established technique of the mature player, is arranged below as a format for each stage in the initial lessons (in italics) set against the general considerations of each aspect of technique (in ordinary type).

Let us assume the pupil to be mid-school age (11–13) possessing a decent student-model instrument. The reed specifications in Chapter 3 are essential.

Producing the first sound

Present the reed without the instrument. The comparative ease of producing a 'crow' on the reed alone will help to avoid the initial inclination to bite it when the resistance of the longer vibrating column of the instrument presents itself. In this way the foundation for a good embouchure may be established immediately. By demonstration show how the lips form a 'cushion' over the teeth. Avoiding any mention of the word 'embouchure', show how the reed is placed centrally on the lower lip (curled around the teeth), the upper lip closing gently on the upper blade. The pupil must be encouraged to think of roundness at the centre of the lips and to barely touch the blade with the upper lip. The reed should only remain firm on the lower lip, where control of the sound rests. At this stage it may be the natural inclination of the pupil to take a breath by lowering the jaw and to breathe between the lower lip and the reed. Therefore, it is best to make clear the necessity for consistent contact between the lower lip and the reed.

Embouchure

For oboists this may be defined as the formation of the lips in supporting the reed and controlling its vibrations. The implications of the word are numerous and may be adapted in as many ways as there are oboists. The meaning of the word can easily become dogmatic if the dangerous view that there is only one way of forming a good embouchure is carried into teaching. Many variable conditions must be considered while outlining general principles: the thickness or otherwise of individual lips; the shape of the jaws; the size and position of the teeth, and the various combinations of all these aspects in individual players.

One feature is constant, and it must be restated. It is the lower lip which asserts the most positive function of control. Therefore, the position of the reed on the lower lip is the most important consideration of all. Placing the blades at measured degrees from the edge of the lip cannot, as some authorities maintain, give a correct position for the reed. Individual characteristics are too variable. The proportion of the reed placed on the lower lip should be judged by the amount of reed left vibrating freely inside the mouth, which amounts to about the length of the tip of the scrape, or 1/16th of an inch. **Plate 11** shows an average lower lip which favours a central position for the reed, midway between the outer edge of the lip and the visible portion of the inside when both lips are relaxed in a normal manner. The lips are then rolled round the teeth and folded with the reed into the mouth, the upper lip closing very gently on the upper blade to seal the embouchure.

Lip control is only achieved after much practice and conditioning of the face muscles, which tire quickly at first in this unnatural position. The intense air pressure which builds up behind the lips when playing into that small crack of an aperture in the reed is a strong factor in tiring both lips and face muscles. The angle at which the oboe is held can affect the ease with which this conditioning can be achieved. If the air being pushed through the reed is constricted in any way by biting too hard on the reed, or by tensing throat muscles in any way, the embouchure is the first condition to feel the strain. **Figure 12** demonstrates one position which may induce this fault: the angle of the oboe causes the reed to point towards the roof of the mouth, which inhibits the easy passage of air into the instrument. We have seen that symmetry in the two blades is the predominant feature of a well-scraped reed. Likewise, the embouchure must achieve a symmetry of upper and lower lips in an equally-poised relationship to the blades. The angle of the instrument will, of course, vary according to the individual physique of jaw shapes. For a person with protruding upper teeth the angle should incline a little more towards the floor. **Figure 13**

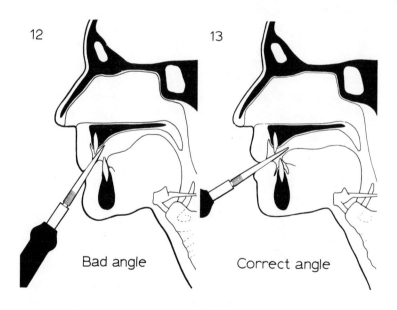

12

13

Bad angle

Correct angle

presents a guideline for the correct angle. Both lips meet at the same point on each blade, creating a firm but supple cushion for the equal vibration of both blades. Also, the reed is directed straight into the line of the air stream. With these factors as a guide, a comfortable position for the angle of the oboe and the position of the reed should be sought by experimentation.

In theory it is desirable to encourage the beginner to articulate the first sound on the reed with a firm 'T'. In practice, however, this is usually more confusing than helpful. After describing the basic function of the lips in forming a cushion between teeth and reed, simply allow the pupil to take most of the cane into the mouth and blow, using analogies such as leaf-blowing to stimulate the idea of a croak. Only then can the natural response of the reed be felt. This achieved, the reed may be withdrawn slightly to create a better situation for the tongue to rest in a convenient position for clear articulation in punctuating the beginning of a note. (The word 'attack' is best avoided with the uninitiated; it encourages an explosive idea for the beginning of a note.) Blowing without the aid of the tongue produces a different physical reaction to the tongued articulation of a sound. Therefore, as soon as the croak is achieved, the tongue should come into play as an agent to the embouchure with the reed being made to speak with the tip of the tongue against the reed.

Tensing of throat muscles has already been described as a constricting situation for sound production. It is possible for this fault to be motivated by the position of the tongue if it is inclined towards the roof of the mouth – especially towards the soft palate at the back, blocking the free passage of air. The tip of the tongue is also important in relation to the embouchure. A relaxed position at the base of the mouth should be maintained as much as possible. The tip can then rest in an easy position against the lower lip, leaving the reed free for the passage of air and the easy manoeuvring of the tongue against the reed for precise articulation.

If all these considerations are implemented the embouchure should feel comfortable and unstrained. Face muscles and throat should feel relaxed and the cavity of the throat open and free for the easy passage of air. In appearance the mirror will not tell you very much, because of the physical variables already discussed. However, at least a small section of the cane should be visible when the embouchure is formed correctly.

When the reed is in the instrument a vast change is made to the forces required for sound production. Initially, the weight of the instrument will incline the pupil to hold it at too low an angle. This will affect the position of the embouchure adversely and should be corrected immediately.

The formation and development of muscular control in the embouchure takes a considerable period of time to mature. Strain and overplaying in the early stages of learning can do harm even to the best potential. Playing for very short intervals, not longer than ten minutes at a time, is as much as the beginner should attempt. The rule is: 'Stop playing when you tire'. Each attempt to play should be preceded by a moment of deep concentration on all the muscular considerations explained above. In this way the pupil's capacity for endurance will develop easily along with the steady progress of other aspects of technique.

While advocating a concept of looseness for a good embouchure I must stress that the variation of lip-pressure is considerable, as will be seen in the discussion of dynamics (p. 81). By 'lip-pressure' I do not mean biting on the lip, but simply increasing the firmness of the lips against the reed according to the dynamics and register which create extremes of response from the instrument; i.e. the lowest notes require the least lip-pressure, while the highest require most. Chapter 9 carries this principle to further extremes in relation to freak notes above the normal range of the instrument. This variability of pressure points towards the instinctive quality a player has to develop in placing a note at the correct pitch, and calculating the degree of lip-pressure required for producing a particular note with a good quality of sound consistent with a homogeneous production over the whole range. In his ballet 'Pulcinella', Stravinsky asks much of this characteristic over a range of two octaves. Between these extremes there is a considerable difference of pressure. Going from a low to a high pressure provides little difficulty for increasing the frequency of a sound; we are on the 'glacier' of a harmonic range which attracts many harmonics, according to the speed of the air entering the vibrating column. Coming from a high to a lower note (especially if both are in the same harmonic series) requires diminution of frequency and less speed of air and air pressure. Compare this with the comparative ease of accelerating in a car to the difficulties of braking to a sudden stop.

In bar 2 of example 2 Stravinsky requires this manoeuvre:

Example 2

Stravinsky: 'Pulcinella'

The frequency of 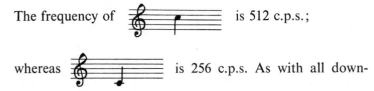 is 512 c.p.s.;

whereas is 256 c.p.s. As with all downward leaps the lower note must be prepared by an embouchure ready to provide the correct lip-pressure to receive this lower frequency. Therefore, play the note at (1) in example 2 with exactly the same loose embouchure required for (2). Exercises with this concept in mind can be found in most of the tutors listed in Appendix 2.

Posture

While attempting the first sounds it is important for the pupil not to be 'blinded with science'. It has already been noted that breath control is a complicated matter to analyse, and any attempt to go into detail about it during the first lesson will undoubtedly be too much for the beginner to digest. Nevertheless, carefully chosen remarks about posture will set the right conditions for good breathing to develop while preparing the pupil for exercises to increase breath-support and control. Observation about posture can be unconsciously absorbed while attention is focused on the embouchure.

Exercise 1. A good posture can be encouraged with the following exercise for the pupil. Standing with back firmly against a wall, with instrument poised for playing, the pupil's head, shoulder-blades, lower back and heels should be pressed firmly against the surface. Playing single notes for variable durations will establish a good position for breath control as well – a subject which requires frequent discussion in many lessons, once the pupil has mastered the elementary details of playing. Generally speaking, pupils should be encouraged to stand as if they are proud of themselves. (See plate 12.)

Good posture affects all facets of technique. The angle recommended for the instrument will not be particularly effective if the rib-cage is constricted by elbows, or the stomach muscles cramped by a lazy seating posture. The whole body is active in controlling the presentation of the sound, so that if any part of the trunk evades a contribution of poise to the general physical posture faults in the production will arise. Elbows should be poised away from the ribs to allow full expansion when a breath is inhaled. Elbows raised too high can be equally inhibiting and ludicrous to look at. A natural curve of the arm from shoulder to hand will provide the best breath and finger control.

Correct balancing of the instrument is imperative before any attempt is made to play it. Most responsibility for this rests with the right hand thumb. Figure 14 shows the correct position with the thumb-rest parallel with the thumb nail. A natural desire to secure a feeling of safety may incline the pupil to support the oboe over the thumb-knuckle. This is dangerous at any stage as it will alter the desired position of the arm in relation to the fingers. We have already noted that the angle of the instrument affects the position of the embouch-

ure. In turn, the correct arm position will support the instrument more naturally and secure good conditions for sustaining a comfortable embouchure.

The left hand index-finger completes the triangle of support for the instrument between the lower lip and the right hand thumb. With the pads of all the fingers resting closely and relaxed near the keys the first note may be sounded with the left hand index-finger (and thumb, if the system adopts a thumb-plate), playing the note b'.

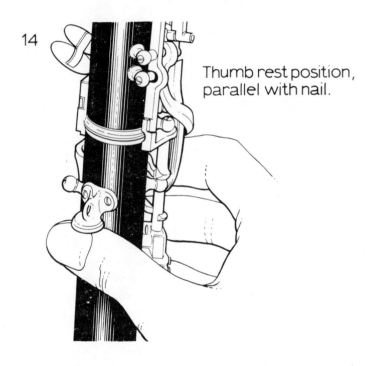

14

Thumb rest position,
parallel with nail.

Many factors in posture may inhibit facility. The most important of all is the relationship of thumb positions to the angle of the arm. This also dictates how the fingers will rest over the keys. If the right hand thumb is inclined to support the oboe with the knuckle behind the thumb-rest, the fingers will be less able to meet the rings and covers of the mechanism with the finger pads. Apart from the fact that this part of the finger is the most sensitive, and therefore able to elicit better control than elsewhere, the fingers work better if bent at the knuckles like levers. The finger pads will only be able to meet the rings comfortably if the thumb is correctly placed at the side of the nail behind the thumb rest. This position is especially important in fork-fingering combinations and trills; the leverage achieved by the bent fingers is more compatible with facility. **Figures 15a** and **15b** may clarify this point.

Other difficulties are encountered with a poor thumb position: elbows tend to be drawn too near to the body; consequently the wrists will be bent as in **fig. 15a.** Such a position will create stiffness from the shoulders to the fingertips. If the shoulders are stiff or, indeed, any of the arm mechanism, the smaller levers of the fingers cannot function freely. **Figure 15b** shows a more natural position with elbows away from the sides creating a regular curve of the whole arm and wrist. **Figure 15c** demonstrates the hand adjustment required to induce this position. **Figure 15d** is correct .

The left hand thumb position is less critical because it does not bear so much of the weight of the instrument as the right hand. The finger-pad touch is, however, equally important.

All fingers should rest gently above the keys, including those for the little fingers of both hands. Pressure should never be used to depress a key. If this is induced by a leaking pad a replacement should be made without delay. Any kind of force required by a finger creates tensions which are invariably passed on to the embouchure and other fingers. Also, on instruments with ring-mechanism rather than covered pads, the steady vibration of the air-column can be disturbed by the air eddies created by a finger thrown hard onto the open hole. This makes a faulty note speak less easily than would a correct light touch.

Special Characteristics Of Basic Fingering Technique

1. $b\flat$–$b\natural$. This is the same for all instruments. Sliding with

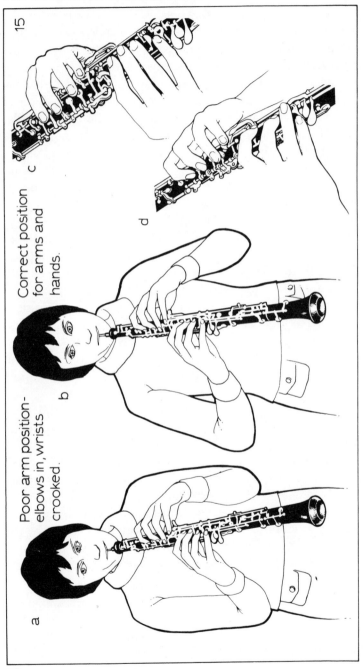

15

Correct position for arms and hands.

Poor arm position - elbows in, wrists crooked.

a

b

c

d

the left hand little finger is the only way to negotiate a slur for these notes. The bent finger 'lever' principle described above is essential. If played with a straight finger the keys will be pressed down at the centre making a slide impossible to negotiate. The bent finger applied at the very edge of the key provides better leverage to secure the closing of the pad at the end of the long rod mechanism. Also, use the lower side of the finger. This enables one to roll the finger on to the adjacent $b\natural$ key with firmness and security. In this way one may retain the looseness and tension-free manipulation which makes for smooth legato and rhythmic precision. $b\natural–b\flat$ should be negotiated in the opposite direction on exactly the same principle. The Trio for Oboe, Bassoon and Piano by Poulenc demands this slur in the slow movement.

2. The 'break' ($c''–c\sharp''$, $c''–d''$). In negotiating a smooth slur between c'' (using only one finger on a thumb-plate system oboe, or two on a Conservatoire model) and $c''\sharp$, using all the fingers of both hands, there are two considerations. (a) Releasing the vent in the left hand index finger-plate. Rolling the index finger on to the plate can be assisted by a downward movement of the wrist which accommodates the second and third fingers in a relaxed, easy motion. Some authorities recommend sliding the index finger. My own preference is for a rolling motion. Perspiration in a hot room can make the plate sticky. Rolling cannot be affected by this contingency, while sliding can be extremely difficult. (b) The accidental 'bagpipe grace', which may easily accompany this interval when slurred, is caused by a lack of co-ordination between the two hands. Usually the fault can be traced to the right hand being lazy. Three or four fingers are required for the $c\sharp''$ (according to the system of the oboe) but only two in the left hand. One may experiment by using the c'' fingering in the left hand, while adding the fingering for $c\sharp''$ in the right hand only. Very little difference will be heard in the pitch of the $c\natural''$. This demonstrates that the right hand should, if anything, move in anticipation of the left when changing to $c\sharp''$, rather than the other way around. Example 3 provides useful practice for this manoeuvre.

Example 3

The cross indicates the use of the right-hand fingering of *c♯″*
with the left hand using only the index-finger. Individual bars
repeated several times using the subsidiary phrase marks may
be balanced by a complete rendering, repeating each bar once
and slurring the whole. The exercise is designed to encourage
anticipation with the right hand for *c♯″*. A smooth, rolling
motion from the wrist should be cultivated with both hands.
Replace *c♯″* with *d″* and *d♯″* to accommodate all situations
relating to the break.

A modification of this approach is found in the Overture of
Mozart's 'Così fan Tutte':

Example 4

Mozart: Overture 'Cosi fan Tutte'.

This is often taken at the very fast pace of ♩ = 150 by many
conductors. In such a situation oscillation over the break is
hazardous. Using the trill key for *d″* is a poor solution because
the thin sound quality and bad intonation of this fingering
will be too apparent in anything slower than a trill. A better
solution relates to the initial bars of example 3. Keep down all
three fingers of the right hand position for *d″* while playing
c″ with authentic left hand fingering.

3. The fully-automatic octave system used on many modern
oboes presents no problems for the interval *g″–a″*, for one

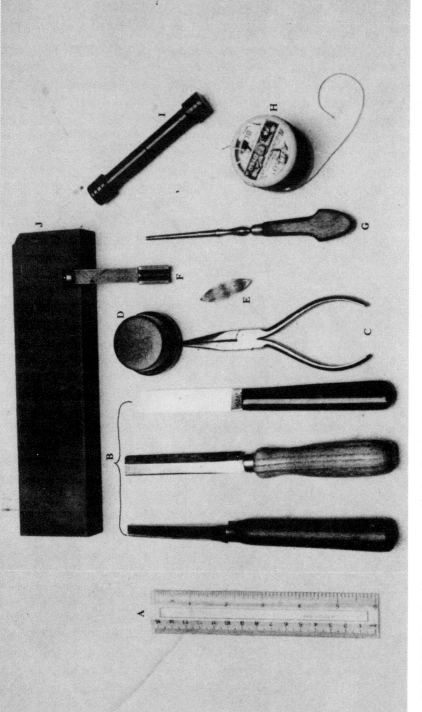

PLATE FIVE Reed-making equipment: (a) ruler; (b) knives for cutting, rough scraping and finishing; (c) pliers; (d) cutting block; (e) scraping tongue; (f) trimmer; (g) binding; (i) barrel; (j) sharpening stone.

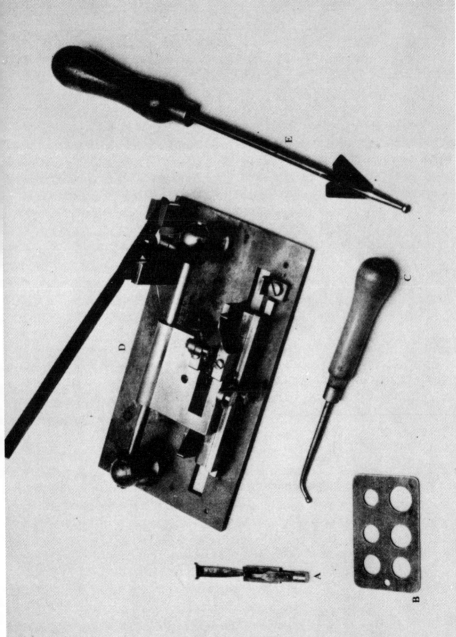

PLATE SIX *Left* (a) shaper; (b) cane measure; (c) gouging handle; (d) gouging machine showing guillotine open; (e) splitter.
PLATE SEVEN *Right below* Pre-gouging bed exposed with cane. *Above* Pushing down plane assembly. (Note the arrows.)

PLATE EIGHT *Above* Gouging. *Below* Scraping.

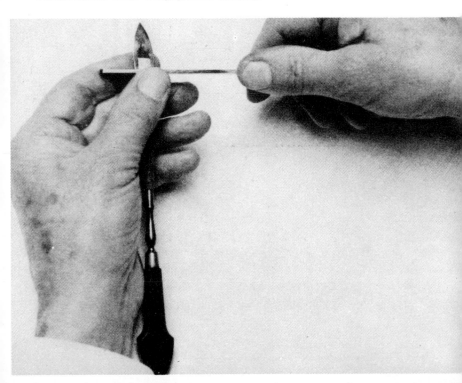

octave key does the work for all speaker notes. The present writer does not favour this kind of mechanism because it limits what we commonly call harmonic fingerings, consequently diminishing the range of colour in the playing. The semi-automatic system employs two speaker keys for different registers: the first from e'' to $g\sharp''$, the second from a'' to c'''. The change from first to second requires a precise action from the left hand. **Plate 13 (a)** shows the hand in the position for g''. **Plate 13 (b)** shows the rocking motion required by the wrist to remove the thumb from the first speaker key, while rocking the index finger onto the knuckle lever of the second speaker key.

Exercises using the rhythms of example 3 will help to develop a smooth, automatic action for this break.

A final observation on the relationship of a good hand position for trills and eighteenth-century shakes. The lever principle for finger positions takes on a special significance here. A free wrist action and a light, relaxed finger touch on the rings and keys are indispensable for lucid, facile ornamentation. The fingering chart (example 5) explains all the finger combinations for trills.

Reliance on the fingers alone will not produce fluency. All trills rely on a gentle, relaxed roll of the wrist – minimal, but enough to assist the individual finger to maintain a rocking motion towards the key. An 'up-and-down' concept can only be maintained by the finger in such a way that no assistance from the wrist and arm can be drawn upon. This generally produces stiff, unsupple finger action which prohibits the lucid performance of trills and graces. The whole of the arm from shoulder to hand requires complete freedom from tension, and a looseness which will allow the rotation of the wrist not only for trills, but for fluency over the breaks, the two octave keys, and all florid passage work.

Exercise 2: To release tension. A basic gymnastic exercise helps in achieving the feeling of complete freedom from tension.

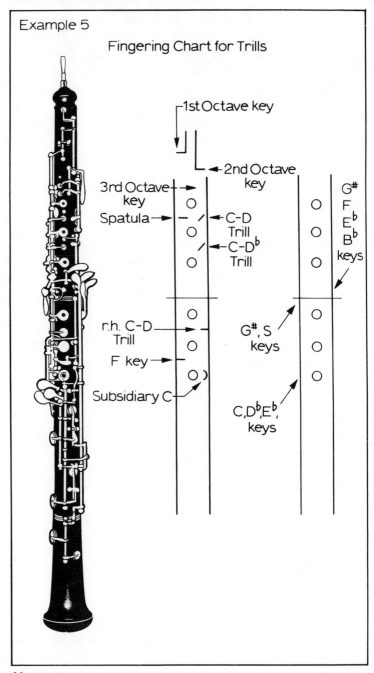

Example 5

Fingering Chart for Trills

1st Octave key

2nd Octave key

3rd Octave key

Spatula

C-D Trill

C-D♭ Trill

G♯ F E♭ B♭ keys

r.h. C-D Trill

F key

Subsidiary C

G♯, S keys

C, D♭, E♭, keys

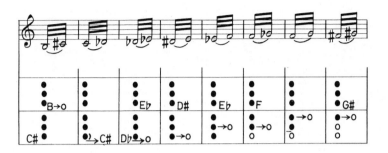

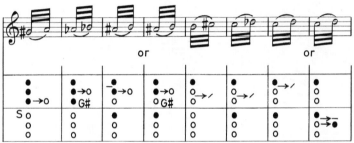

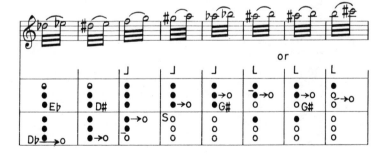

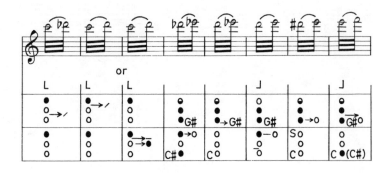

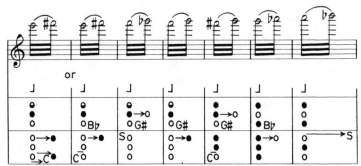

(Teeth emboucher)

1. Simply swing both arms around in circles from front to back several times, windmill fashion.

2. Then drop both arms to the sides loosely and shake arms and hands as fast as possible in a rotating manner in the same spot. (The right hand tires quicker than the left after a long period of sustained playing. Players with small hands are likely to suffer more from the weight of the instrument.) This exercise improves circulation and relaxes the tendons and muscles in performance.

Scales

The fact that all Western music up to 1900, and much of it after this date, was based on the diatonic scale, is perhaps sufficient qualification for the immense importance of scale practice in developing a reliable technique. Tutors and study volumes listed in Appendix 2 provide a catalogue of variable formations and practice methods. However, it is not enough to begin and end on the tonic, for music often demands the use of a more licentious rhythmic structure than this basic pivot can offer. Example 6 demonstrates one possibility for ringing the changes of rhythmic stress in scale practice.

Example 6

Scales

Arpeggios

* It is the weaker intervals that require astringent control in several different rhythmic displacements within one phrase. Eugène Bozza carries this to an extreme in his '14 Studies in Karnatic Modes'. They are based on twenty-four different Indian modes and nine rhythmic structures, which cover many aspects of finger control not normally negotiated in standard scale-playing methods.

In slow-moving pieces requiring a tenuous *legato* line, any tendency to move the fingers slowly at the change of each note should be avoided. It is a natural inclination stimulated by the character of such a piece. Throughout *legato* passages of this kind, fingers should depress the keys as rapidly and as lightly as in a fast movement, leaving the change as late as possible. With firm breath-support this will enhance the *legato* and avoid sluggish phrasing and fingering. The quick movement of the fingers should actively belie the smoothness of the resulting flow of sound.

Breath Control

The physiology of respiration requires a brief explanation in order to clarify the function of the system in controlling the sound. Inhaling is an involuntary action. We breathe in almost without being conscious of it. The thoracic cavity which contains the lungs is framed by the ribs, the sternum (breast bone), the vertebral column and the diaphragm. Being able to move they provide the mechanism for the swelling and diminishing of the cavity. When a breath is taken in, two things happen: the ribs move upwards and the diaphragm moves down. The latter is a tough, muscular partition shaped like a dome which separates the chest from the abdomen. It contracts with inhalation and the dome becomes flat. At the same time the ribs are raised and, naturally, the chest capacity is increased. The descent of the diaphragm pushes the abdominal wall forward by the increased pressure.

Breathing out is not so automatic. It can be done either actively or passively. In the case of wind-players it is of course active, involving the use of the muscles of the abdominal wall. By contracting, they increase the pressure which forces the diaphragm upwards back towards the chest. The part played by the chest wall and the diaphragm will vary considerably from one person to another. It is especially important when analysing the muscular basis of breath control to bear in mind that women depend much more than men on the chest wall, whereas men have a naturally stronger reliance on the diaphragm. Therefore, it is a mistake to consider that everything depends on the diaphragm alone in substantiating the muscular support behind the blowing. This is primarily abdominal for both sexes.

Awareness of the breathing mechanism is important to the oboist in cultivating muscular control of these reactions. Contraction of the abdominal muscles is the positive physical assertion which determines the continued pressure of air passing into the instrument. It is a reaction which requires the ability to isolate mentally the abdominal area of one's body, so that all other physical conditions remain free from tension when conscious flexing of the abdominal muscles for blowing takes place. Pushing the air in this way provides the most important aspect of tone quality; for without the strength of this support other muscles automatically come into play which induce tension, and a poor, 'squeezed' tone. The firmness of the tone produced from a correct abdominal control is clearly manifested in performance. Simply blowing hard or soft will give a consistently good quality in all extremes of dynamic range if the support remains constant.

Even this brief explanation of breath support should make clear the importance of good posture, especially when sitting to play in an orchestra. Any inclination to slump will create tensions which easily interfere with the activity of the breathing muscles. Physical exertion must be restricted as much as possible to the muscles described if tension is to be avoided. These conditions become even more significant in relation to the passage of air through the throat. We have already discovered that without abdominal support, throat muscles involuntarily become tense in an effort to push the air into the instrument. If the diaphragm conditions are correct, keeping an open throat will not be a problem. The open throat cavity, and indeed the relaxed tongue position are further agents in producing a full tone quality.

Although breath control needs much discussion in several lessons, the fundamental conditions set out above survey the essential conditions for tone production. A factual discussion, however, cannot necessarily convey true comprehension of the feeling which results when correct control is achieved. The following remarks and exercises are directed towards implementing productive muscular control over a long period of time – for time is required for muscles to develop a consistent response to the demands of oboe playing.

Inhaling

The aim is to achieve a breathing technique which fills the bottom of the lungs, for this is where active control of breath support rests. Restricted use of the upper intercostal muscles is an active agent in increasing endurance and control; therefore, they should remain inactive. Tensing the abdominal muscles in isolation from the thoracic cavity is not easy for the beginner to achieve.

Exercise 3: The pupil should stand upright with head up straight. Hold both arms akimbo, then place both hands on the back of the rib cage as high up as possible, thumbs facing the front, and the four fingers splayed out across the back of the rib-cage, as in **fig. 16.** Pull shoulders as far back as possible. This position restricts the activity of the intercostal muscles of necessity. The tension across the top of the rib

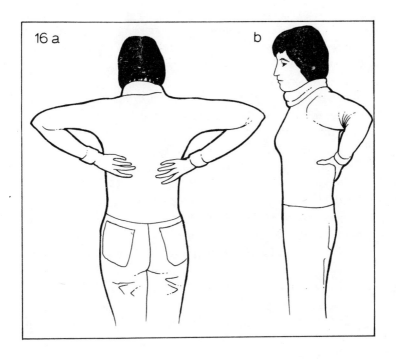

cage is so great that when a breath is taken, expansion at this point will be minimal. If the pupil takes in a breath with the notion of trying to breath with the stomach, the essential lower part of the rib-cage will expand, automatically inducing the deep, low breathing required. He/she will also be able to feel the expansion of the rib-cage at the back with the hands, as well as the taut feeling of expansion at the front. Deep breaths in this position before each practice session help to achieve the correct feeling for the development of this functional muscular habit, which may be compared to the reaction we feel when coughing or clearing the throat.

Actors use an exercise for voice projection which oboists

73

can usefully adopt for breathing. It is ideal for achieving control of abdomen muscles, and producing strong support beneath the diaphragm.

Exercise 4: Take a breath in the position of exercise 3. Imagine you are about to enter a room full of feathers, then drop your arms to the sides and purse your lips. Entering such a room you would want to avoid breathing-in the feathers. Through pursed lips blow repeatedly through the smallest aperture you can produce at the centre of the lips. The sharp contraction of the abdomen muscles is very powerful indeed. Placing a hand below the ribs will emphasize the reaction.

Exercises 3 and 4 present the correct sensation for abdominal support in short, sharp reactions. Once understood, this should be applied in a longer, sustained situation. **Exercise 5** *presents a rhythmic motive which will stimulate the consistent support required in all performing circumstances.*

Blow the rhythms with pursed lips, as in exercise 4.

Exercise 5

Detailed discussion of breath control is best started when the pupil is able to maintain embouchure control for the performance of a single-octave scale. Exercises on each interval of a scale, using one of the note patterns of example 3 (page 64), will encourage the force of projection required.

Singers are often observed in their exercises with mouth wide open and left hand performing a coaxing sweep from the mouth to an invisible audience. Far from any melodramatic intention, this exercise is a valuable gesture which helps the singer to become diaphragm conscious. It cultivates exactly the same kind of support and projection which the wind-player seeks. This is a valuable example for the oboist because it focuses the importance of cavity resonance. The singer must keep an open and relaxed throat for exactly the same reasons as the oboist; but the singer has the advantage of being able to produce the sound with an open mouth. Nevertheless, this yawning sensation is exactly the kind of feeling which the oboist must cultivate as early as possible. For the more advanced pupil with an established embouchure, cultivation of projection, along with sound quality, can be improved by further inducement of the open throat function.

Exercise 6: *Using a fairly shallow embouchure (i.e. withdrawing the reed to play at its tip) sing and play at the same time. To do this one has to yawn on the sound and superimpose the oboe tone on to the voice. All the aspects of abdominal support and freedom from tension must be correct to produce this 'double-sound'. Thus the exercise has the dual purpose of assisting abdominal support, or demonstrating its absence, if singing and playing at the same time cannot be achieved.*

It sometimes happens that a gifted student can develop a high degree of competence as an oboist, but maintains a poor production based on a badly-formed embouchure. Tightness and biting are syndromes with which the teacher must constantly battle. Often it can be that the student has used reeds that are too hard in the early stages of learning, and poor habits have developed in the effort to combat the too strong resistance of the reed. This situation undoubtedly implies a stiff embouchure with little or no abdominal support of the breath.

Exercise 7: *With a free and responsive reed the pupil's jaw can be slackened by playing as flat as possible – if necessary, to the point of absurdity at first. Automatically this will release the stiffness of the lower lip and jaw, being the only possible way of producing a flat pitch under normal circumstances. While doing this the pupil should try to correct the pitch by pushing more air into the instrument. In other words, the unbalanced relationship of embouchure and diaphragm in the pupil's faulty production is now inverted. The abdominal support has to compensate for the slackness of embouchure which excessively flat playing will induce.*

Articulation and Attack

In speech, articulation refers to the joining of syllables by consonants. Wind-players adopt the word to define the action required for joining notes by the use of a consonant which interrupts the continuity of sound with varying degrees of separation. The tongue is the only agent that can perform this function. How we use it in oboe-playing is a vital part of tone production. Eighteenth-century performers considered the variable forms of articulation as the most important aspect of phrasing and characterization. Fundamentally this has not changed. Complete control of this function depends on the position of the tongue in relation to the reed. In talking and singing we unconsciously sustain a constant supply of air while articulating consonants as well as vowels. With the exception of the diphthong all syllables use both, and we do not switch off the air supply demanded of the vocalized vowels when joining them with consonants.

All this is very elementary. But not so when we adopt the unnatural position formed by the embouchure when an oboe reed is in the mouth. On the principles described in our discussion of breath control we must consciously sustain the supply of air with the extra pressure demanded to make the reed sound.

The conditions required of the tongue in supplying the articulation of the sound are derived from a very relaxed position at the base of the mouth with tip resting under the reed, just touching the curled lower lip. To articulate, raise the tongue gently but quickly towards the reed, tipping the lower blade very gently using a place just behind the upper tip of the tongue. Think of a gentle 'T' as the basis for this articulation. Breath-support must accompany this action as the 'T' is pronounced, and is, of course, continued after the withdrawal of the tongue.

In early lessons the pupil will benefit from an analogous description of the basic form of articulation:

Think of the tongue as a gate against the aperture of the reed. From behind the gate a constant pressure of air is push-ing against the upper teeth – that is, the abdominal pressure on the diaphragm is continually asserted. When the gate is opened, and the tongue withdrawn below the reed, the air rushes in without resistance. When the note is to stop, the gate is closed as the tongue is placed against the reed again. The pressure of air must remain constant. In this way the danger of an explosive attack by too strong an articulation of the tongue is avoided. The articulation may be thought of in terms of tongue withdrawal rather than attack.

By thinking of an up-and-down motion for the attack, explosive articulation will be avoided. The 'T' will then present *itself* rather than be asserted by a forward throw on to the reed. Lightness of tongue follows all other facets of controlled technique in the evasion of tenseness and rigidity. The breath support behind this action should remain constant for all extremes of dynamics. Contact of the lower lip and the underside of the tongue tip will provide adequate support for the easiness of tongue motion and prevent the smothered attack ('ther') which derives from the tongue meeting both blades head on for an articulation.

Withdraw the tongue from the reed to start a note; replace it to finish. The replacing action, however, is not necessary if a breath is to be taken before a subsequent articulation. The smallest action possible is required of the tongue in all this. Ultimately, it may be found that 'T' becomes more like 'D' in achieving a clean attack. This is desirable. 'T' after all, creates a rush of air when we articulate, encouraging the explosive attack we would wish to avoid. 'D' represents the action of releasing the tongue from the reed, and, if well supported by the breath, will present a neat and cleanly-attacked note.

The less the tongue has to move to articulate the better. A 'spongy' tone quality can often be traced to a tongue position which makes the attack directly in front of the reed, causing the tongue to roll back into the throat afterwards. This will distort the air-stream and stifle the easy production of the sound. The breath must always maintain an independent function from the tongue if ease and clarity of articulation are to be achieved.

For *staccato* playing and any highly articulated phrases, less air passes through the instrument at any given time than with sustained sound. Positive restraint of breath will help ease of articulation in such passages. The length of staccato notes may vary considerably from piece to piece. 'T' is the best consonant for this purpose because it provides an immediate projection of the breath into the instrument. The faster the music, the lighter the tongue must be in its action against the reed. There is a real danger of this important characteristic of oboe-playing becoming distorted. A 'quacking' sound will easily result from too heavy an action of the tongue, and too short a note. In other words the sound may easily acquire heavy articulation and little tone, as if a speaker were clipping the vowels and over-emphasizing all the consonants. It is a useful consideration to define the word '*staccato*' in its literal definition, 'detached.' It is all too easy to think of it as a 'short as possible' articulation. The note must have substance, no matter how short the *staccato*.

To postulate a definitive form of *staccato* would encourage a style of playing based on mannerisms. Each work employing such passages should be judged in relation to its individual expressive requirements. The choice of various forms of *staccato* also takes into account the possibilities of using double- and triple-tonguing. Before examining musical examples, a few brief words on these two forms of quick tonguing:

Double-Tonguing

Two consonants are used which employ different parts of the tongue: 'TER' and 'KER'. 'T' at the tip in the usual position; 'K', using the part of the tongue which produces the consonant in a natural kind of position meeting the roof of the mouth just in front of the soft palate. It is easier to control at very fast speeds than those which can normally be negotiated by single-tonguing.

Triple-Tonguing

According to the rhythm of the piece three forms may be

used: TER-TER-KER; TER-KER-TER; TER-KER-TER| KER-TER-KER.

Some players use double and triple-tonguing consistently. There is no hard and fast rule about this. The individual jaw, teeth and mouth formation will dictate to a player which form is best. My own experience tells that any method adopted, providing the sound produced fulfils the requirements of lucid, expressive articulation, will be satisfactory. For most of my life I have rarely used double- and triple-tonguing, for I have felt firmer control from the development of my single-tonguing. However, since the re-formation of my embouchure, following an accident, I have used double-tonguing far more than ever before.

Rossini provides the best standard examples of fast tonguing and *staccato* playing; all oboists will consider the Overture 'The Silken Ladder' one of the more exacting solos a player may face (example 7).

Example 7

Rossini: 'The Silken Ladder' Overture

If the player chooses to double-tongue the passage, care must be taken to avoid over-accentuation of the TER at the expense of the KER. All the quavers must be equally balanced in length and dynamic level. With single-tonguing

79

attempts to play the quavers too short will necessitate more action from the tongue. The piece travels so fast that all one needs to consider is separation. Approach it with a *legato* concept, then consider the separation of notes with the lightest possible 'up-and-down' tonguing on the corner of the tip of the reed. Full diaphragm support should be constant to substantiate the sound, and no breaths may be contemplated. The passage lasts 17–18 seconds, but may seem longer in execution. Psychologically, the estimated duration of such a passage can provide a further source of confidence and relaxation. The penultimate bar of example 7 exposes a characteristic which occurs in many works: tonguing bottom notes rapidly. As you approach this bar allow the upper lip to cover the reed a little more than usual, and the lower lip to recede slightly. Apart from allowing the tongue to move more easily, it permits an easier attack when the tongue may be tiring. The orchestra generally covers the last five notes of the piece. Do not allow this to make you play louder. Throughout the entire solo, avoid any attempt to play more than a good, projected *mezzo-forte*. The louder one tries to play the more sluggish the articulation will become because of the greater resistance met from the instrument and reed in this low register.

Example 8, 'The Barber of Seville' (Act III) provides an

Example 8

Rossini *The Barber of Seville*

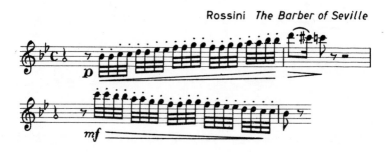

important solo for the oboe in which double-tonguing is almost indispensable. In attempting it with single-tonguing, articulation should be approached with TER-RE in mind. Think of it as single semi-quavers without the reiterated note, before attempting the light tip needed with the -RE articulation.

For other forms of *staccato* tonguing, see example 9, from Mozart's Concerto, and example 10, from the Scherzo of Beethoven's Ninth Symphony.

Example 9

Mozart *Concerto*

Example 10

Beethoven *Symphony No.9 (Scherzo)*

Dynamics

It has to be admitted that the oboe, like the other reed instruments, has a comparatively limited expressive range. Strings can soar away over several octaves, and double-stop; they possess a wide range of variable harmonics and tone textures, various forms of articulation; the figurative field of variation is endless, and the repertoire . . . !

This is not to say that the oboe is a poor relation; it is simply admitting to its limitations. Starting from this point of view the performer can approach his instrument with an attitude of determination to develop every expressive agent the oboe possesses to its ultimate extreme. Perhaps the most important of all characteristics in this range is dynamic control. There are few experiences more boring than an oboe recital by a player with too small a range of dynamic variation. From Prokofiev's quacking duck in 'Peter and the Wolf' to Sibelius's shimmering 'Swan of Tuonela' the oboe family can adapt to many forms of characterization. But without a wide range of dynamic control a performance can pall.

In seeking such control the quality of the tone must remain constant. To achieve this, the embouchure and the abdomen support share responsibility, for it is not enough simply to blow harder for *forte* and softer for *piano*. Indeed, the quietest note possible requires as much abdominal support as the loudest of notes if one is to sustain a good, firm quality of tone. That is not to say that we should blow as energetically for a soft sound as for a loud, but that the urge to *support* the sound should be even greater for a soft tone because the air pressure of the stream is less.

The natural position for the embouchure should provide a degree of lip mobility. With the lower lip placed in the position advised it should be possible, when attempting a *diminuendo*, to withdraw the reed slightly without changing the place of the reed on the lips. This means that the small area of the reed tip vibrating freely in the mouth comes more in direct contact with the lower lip curled around the bark. In other words, the easy vibration of the tip is smothered slightly by the lips, thus increasing the resistance of the reed by dampening it. This can also have the undesired effect of sharpening a note. Combat this by establishing an initial position at the tip of the reed.

A good *diminuendo* will often finish with the sound literally expiring into silence – as, indeed, a note may begin from silence. While sustaining firm abdominal support throughout the quietest sounds, it is well to bear in mind that it is air in the instrument that produces the sound; therefore, abdominal support must remain constant.

Example 11

Brahms *Symphony No. 1*

espr.

cresc.

Example 11 provides a good test of dynamic control. As the first solo entry in the slow movement Brahms has declined from providing a dynamic mark. The oboist begins alone, deriving a dynamic from the level of the previous phrase by the sonorous full strings. Although the melody beseeches the oboist to play with a full, rich sound, enough reserve must be found for the height of the phrase at the b'', when full woodwind and strings meet the climax with a restatement of the main first subject in expressive counterpoint. Musically, it is untenable to consider taking a breath. The dotted crotchet at X (where it might be assumed reasonable to snatch a breath for the climax) cannot be released because the resolution of the diminished seventh demands the sustained presence of the b''. The horns, who also sound a B, are playing in the wrong register to leave it solely to them; they require the complementary presence of the solo line. After the glorious climax of the phrase the last three quavers of the melody fall considerably in the *diminuendo* to the g♯, then to the violins' f♯' in the next bar, where the bassoon joins them, *pianissimo*, to complete the phrase. The separated articulations of the three notes preceding the b'' are sensitively acknowledged by Brahms to be in the hands of the oboist's artistry as slightly more emphatic in their legato-tonguing, rather than slurred, as in the previous bars.

Dynamics make or break such a beautiful phrase. The projected *piano* of the beginning must sing above the swelling accompanying phrases without rising and falling with them, so that when the crescendo is accomplished on the b'' the spaciousness and dignity of the line remain undisturbed as the climax is reached. (Further discussion of projecting the upper range can be found on pp. 139–40 in relation to the Mozart Concerto.)

The upper register of the oboe can sound rather thin between a'' and c''' because most of the finger-holes are open, leaving the length of closed-pipe resonance very short. A perfectly legitimate way of giving more substance to notes like the b'' in example 11 is to close certain holes at the bottom of the instrument as follows:

Figure 17

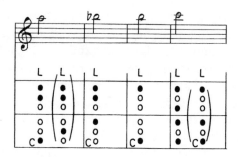

These fingerings have the effect of providing extra resonance to the greater length of closed pipe, giving added lustre and projection to the sound.

Dynamic range is a vitally important element of phrasing, yet it is an area which easily induces mannerisms more than any other. Idiosyncratic editions by some oboists demonstrate this fact with 'hairpin' *crescendi* and *diminuendi* in the most unlikely places, more often than not at the end of every phrase. In an attempt to achieve contrast of dynamic range it is an easy pitfall to encounter. The colloquial word for it is 'bulging'. For oboists it is as good a piece of onomatopoeia as can be found, because it describes the mannerisms in uncomplimentary fashion. Example 12, from the same Brahms Symphony, easily invites it if the player is unaware of the danger.

Example 12

Brahms: Symphony No. 1

The persistent reiteration of the *g'* in the first two bars sometimes on, sometimes off the beat, encourages unintended stresses which derive from the nature of the instrument rather than the composer's idea.

Two dangers are present. First, the necessity to slur down to the *g'* requires embouchure preparation each time, and bulging can occur as an unconscious reaction to slackened lips. Secondly, in an attempt to avoid such a situation the opposite can occur. The dynamics in parenthesis show alternate notes between the *g*'s becoming stressed. Ultimately it is what can only be described as a sense of line which matters most in the dynamic shaping of such phrases. Again, the embouchure must remain loose, and breath-support strong to carry the steady crescendo towards the climax of the phrase on *d'''*.

Throughout the early stages of playing the pupil should always be encouraged to play with a full tone. In developing control of muscles for embouchure and breath-support a sense of vigour will encourage the maturing of control and projection. Even the quietest pianissimo in a solo must be heard at the back of the concert hall, which implies that a strong, firm sound must be the basis for all extremes of dynamics. Once the embouchure can sustain control for lengthy periods, the time will have come to develop dynamic nuance in the playing. The best approach is age-old and cannot be bettered. Chromatic and diatonic scales can be used with the following formula:

Exercise 8

Begin a note with all the conditions of good embouchure, breath control and articulation in mind. **Exercise 8** *can be varied in tempo and dynamics. For instance: begin* ppp *and crescendo to* fff, *then back to* ppp. *Apart from stimulating control of the whole dynamic range, this exercise focuses the necessity for mobility of embouchure from one dynamic field to another. In order to sustain a steady pitch for each note from* ppp *to* fff *the embouchure must involve withdrawal of the lips from the mouth and a looser sense of contact towards the tip of the reed. Assertion of the concept of full abdominal support for quiet as well as loud notes is very important here and stresses the necessity for individual control of embouchure and abdomen support. While breath support remains constant throughout the exercise, the embouchure must gradually withdraw from the stifled attack needed for* ppp *to a fully relaxed lower lip, withdrawn to allow the tip of the reed to vibrate more freely in the mouth. If these considerations are ignored the result is a gradual sharpening of pitch towards the* fff. *The value of the exercise rests in the necessity to combine all elements of good playing already discussed with the added requirement of sustaining correct pitch throughout all the changes of muscular assertion. For the beginner it is the most important of all basic exercises for developing firm control of the sound.*

Tone Quality

The quality of sound produced depends on two major factors: (1) the accepted basic sound of the country or region in which the player lives; (2) the personal taste of the individual oboist. Both of these aspects will dictate the kind of scrape the player uses. In their excellent book Sprenkle and Ledet give pointers to a widely accepted form of V shape scrape used by many American players, which dispenses with most of the bark of the cane in a similar fashion to those of Viennese players. They create a rich, heavy sound which suits Viennese oboes especially well.

A further influence in America was the long domicile of Tabuteau in Philadelphia as a teacher. Two generations of American players have come under his influence. America is a large country and it would be fatuous to suppose that each State would necessarily adopt a blueprint style of reed. Nevertheless, the rich, woody quality we associate with much recorded American playing has a distinctive quality which has much to do with the V scrape. France and most of Europe incline more towards the U scrape which provides a lighter and sweeter sound.

Vibrato

The kind of scrape used has a very assertive effect on the singing quality of the tone, especially in one exceptionally important facet – that of *vibrato*. The soul of the sound can justifiably be said to rest in this quality. Yet attitudes towards its use have varied considerably throughout history.

As I explained earlier, the fashionable woodwind sound in the early days of this century was more wooden. *Vibrato* was rarely, if ever used, and certainly not as a fundamental aspect of tone production. Those first days at the Queen's Hall Orchestra represented for me a period of isolation from the prevalent style of sound reproduction. I suffered a great deal of abuse and jibing from other players at this time for persisting with my own concept of a beautiful oboe sound incorporating *vibrato* as an essential aspect of its singing quality. However, critics were favourably disposed and conductors liked it; so my confidence in the approach was ultimately justified.

Vibrato is a quality which defies close analysis in any useful sense, nor indeed can it be induced by exercises and explanations. If all the physical conditions of good playing along with freedom from tension are achieved, *vibrato* becomes an expressive inflection of musical personality and sensibility.

Part Two: The Reed and the Oboist

The physical reaction fundamental to real control may be thought of as an undulation of wind pressure rather than rapid changes of frequency:

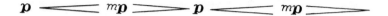

Any attempt to produce it by varying the pitch of a note (frequency) will create a quacking sound. It is the most natural thing in the world to do, and our constant analogy with singing is the best example to follow. In excess it is distasteful.

Muscular control of *vibrato* relies on the abdominal support of the diaphragm. The mobility of the embouchure will occasionally induce a minimal lip movement in slow melodies; but real control rests with the diaphragm. Sensitivity to the response of the instrument and reed presents the natural capacity to indulge the tone quality with a *vibrato* which can be harnessed to an expressive inflection. One should be able to switch it on or off according to the character of the music, as well as being able to determine the speed of the cycles. With careful listening it may be judged that 5–7 cycles per second is the only effective gauge to use; a faster speed would make the sound of an organ 'tremulant' stop; slower, it would create a distortion of tone which may sound like a written-out rhythmic figuration on the note. So within this small scale of variable cycles a wide area of musical characterization can be achieved with the use of *vibrato*. A few examples will illustrate these possibilities.

No Vibrato

Example 13

Ravel: Beginning of 'Daphnes et Chloé' Part I

Example 13 is the beginning of Part I of Ravel's 'Daphnes et Chloé'. The setting of this moment establishes the nature of the whole ballet. The scene at the beginning depicts a clear afternoon in spring. The oboe motiv underlays the plaintive pipe of the god Pan, whose archaic form can be seen vaguely in the shape of a rock. The awakening spirit of the god is evoked in each note like a ghostly echo across the centuries. *Vibrato* is out of the question!

Being the first note the oboe plays in the piece, this entry can be hazardous. The long f''' fingering is more secure than the short f''' on most instruments. (See Appendix 3 for fingering chart.) Here, it is vital to prepare the note with more reed than usual in the mouth, asserting abdominal support before the note is attacked. A loose embouchure and lots of air in the instrument will add clarity to the attack and avoid the possibility of an explosive accent. The reiteration of each f''' will be lost if the notes are not separated sufficiently. Sustain strong abdominal support, but use the tongue against the reed to stop the flow of air between each articulation.

Intonation is also a hazard in this solo. By taking more reed in the mouth for a secure attack on the first f''' it is easy to overdo it, making the $c\sharp'''$ and e''' too sharp. These are sharp notes on most oboes and require embouchure adjustment by withdrawing the reed a little from the mouth. Variations on the right-hand fingering can adjust this without too much necessity for a change of embouchure. Ideally, it is best to set the embouchure with a minimal adjustment for the first f''' and rely on abdominal support. The $e\flat'''$ at the end of the phrase is quite a different matter, however. *ppp* on this note, after a diminuendo, is rather an unkind demand from Ravel, but produces an incomparably beautiful effect if done well. Reducing the aperture of the reed with a firmer embouchure is necessary – but damaging to the pitch, unless compensating adjustment is made elsewhere. Accept that it will be sharp. Combat this by using 'long' fingering with the addition of right hand middle finger to flatten the note.

Slow Vibrato

Example 14

Slow movement

Example 14, from the slow movement of Brahms's Violin Concerto, must be one of the best-loved and most beautiful of all orchestral oboe solos. The warmth of a slow *vibrato* is an essential part of the tone-quality for the piece. The beauty of its rendering inculcates every aspect of technique discussed in this chapter and needs no further explanation, except with regard to one point – the tongued semi-*legato* notes of bar 2 and similar phrases throughout the solo. Violinists would take both semiquavers with one bow, stopping it very briefly between the two notes. The tongue must serve the same function for the oboist. Perhaps our 'singer' comparison would serve to explain even more clearly. Suppose the melody to be set to the words 'dans la mer'. The singer would elide the three words without any consonant interruption of the sound. Using a gentle 'der-der' attack with the tongue, think of 'dans la' on the two semiquavers, and the semi-*legato* phrasing will become self-evident. The sound is continuous except for the lightest and gentlest punctuation with the tongue. This is especially important at bars 15–16 through the *crescendo* to c‴′. Here the *vibrato* can be intensified to match the emotional heightening of the phrase; then relax again to the original, to colour the serenity of the closing bars. The slow speed of the *vibrato* will help to add spaciousness to the movement of the quavers. Semiquavers, too, need to 'fill the beat' almost to the point of being behind the conductor.

Medium Vibrato

Example 15

Delius *La Calinda*

Example 15, from Delius' 'La Calinda', requires this most basic form of *vibrato* and should be thought of as an intrinsic part of fundamental tone quality. The example chosen is an open-throated song; perhaps one of the most beautiful melodies ever written for the oboe. Difficulties sometimes arise when slurring from *a♯″* to *d♯‴*. The trouble can generally be resolved by reed adjustment. Either the tip is too long, or the aperture too open. Remedies are discussed in Chapter 3.

Fast Vibrato

Example 16

This form of *vibrato* can be most appropriately applied in the vigorous and playful music of the classical era, and the early twentieth-century French composers. The vibrant, fast *vibrato* is nearest to the quality adaptable to the classical oboe, which aims at brilliance and panache. Example 16 is taken from the last movement of Mozart's Sinfonia Concertante for Violin and Viola.

Combination of Fast and Slow Vibrato

Example 17

Example 17, from the slow movement of Schubert's 'Unfinished' Symphony, demonstrates the combination of two kinds of *vibrato* within one phrase. We have already seen how Mozart contains several figurative characterizations within a single phrase, which constantly varies the form of articulation and manner of phrasing. In the Schubert example the variety of phrase character which can be emphasized by different kinds of vibrato is manifest. The first six bars call for the slow *vibrato* of the Brahms Violin Concerto, whereas bars 7 and 8 require the more lyrical quality of the Delius example.

Categorizing various forms of *vibrato* may seem dogmatic if I avoid adding a general observation. 'Turning the knob' for a particular form is not a useful concept. But by setting out specific possibilities of expressive application, one can be more conscious of the variety of possibilities available to colour the phrasing of each piece tackled. There are an infinite number of possibilities which affect the interpretation of a piece. The freshness of each performance can only be maintained if the artist is continually exploring alternative avenues of nuance and expression. Discriminating use of *vibrato* can be the most valuable of assets in these discoveries.

Tone Quality of the Cor Anglais

It is easier to produce a pleasing quality of sound on the cor anglais than on the oboe because the response is made easier by the larger size of reed and bore. The deeper register helps to enrich the sound by providing the velvety glow which we associate with the tone. The only important difference between the playing techniques of the two instruments lies with the use of *vibrato*. In general it must be slower on the cor anglais, with fewer possibilities of variation, especially of the quicker kind. It is very easy to make this instrument bleat. Its basic characteristics are less variable than the oboe, therefore its role in the orchestra is limited more to the specific representation of stylized solos. This is well demonstrated in Stravinsky's 'Rite of Spring', where the cor anglais is almost exclusively the main soloist of the oboe section throughout the work. The use of *vibrato* may be observed at its two extremes in the following examples:

Part Two: The Reed and the Oboist

Example 18

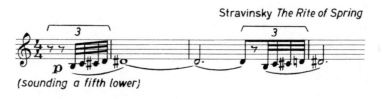

Stravinsky *The Rite of Spring*

(sounding a fifth lower)

Example 19

Sibelius *The Swan of Tuonela*

(sounding a fifth lower)

Example 18 accompanies the foreboding 'Ritual Action of the Elders', which immediately precedes the final 'Sacrificial Dance', when the chosen one must dance herself to death. All the primitive awakening of an inexorable ritual, of a relentless mystical purpose is insidiously evoked in this oily motiv. *Vibrato*? No!

Example 19 is, on the contrary, a serene and vivid portrait of beauty. No instrument has ever inspired a more apposite gem of poetic imagery than the cor anglais in this work. The natural, pure tone of the instrument must speak in every bar with the shades of a relaxed and sensitively regulated *vibrato*.

In practising and performing these works, the cor anglais player will enhance his oboe playing. Any myth to the contrary should be ignored.

Part Three

The Music

Five

Playing Baroque Music
(by Edwin Roxburgh)

The Problem

'With one who has thoroughly mastered his art, we are on safer ground than with one who has only followed his good instincts.'

Quantz, writing in 1752, could have made such a statement today with equal relevance and wisdom. As a result of avid research, along with the increasing availability of old sources in published versions and translations, today's performers are faced with a much wider area of stylistic considerations than ever before. The weight of information and the accessibility of good reproduction baroque instruments has created a new and specialized field of development in performing. It is a matter of serious concern that if we play eighteenth-century music on a modern oboe we are, in fact, playing it on a different instrument from the one for which the music was originally written. The baroque oboe requires an entirely different concept of playing.

How then, do we approach the performing of baroque and classical music on the modern oboe with the thought that the music was composed for another instrument? What were the essential qualities of the old instruments, and how can we best relate them to modern conditions? The distinguishing characteristics are well-documented by eighteenth-century composers and makers such as Jacques Hotteterre and Quantz:

1. According to the latter, the baroque oboe was much quieter and softer in tone quality and therefore not as penetrating or capable of the strident qualities of the modern instrument.

2. Hotteterre explains the complex correlations between articulation and phrasing, demonstrating far more subtlety than is often credited to baroque performing.

97

3. Garnier tells us that *vibrato* was produced by shaking the lips (*fremissement*), quite contrary to modern practice.

4. Prelleur describes the formation of the embouchure, recommending the player to 'press the reed between your lips almost close together'. This is to accommodate the overblowing technique in the absence of our present day octave key – and is bad advice for the modern oboist!

5. Tone quality is very much characterized by the boxwood used for making all oboes up to the 19th century.

The absence of keys and the great importance which Quantz attaches to the varieties of tone colour and intonation by cross-fingering techniques, along with the much broader gouge and shape of the reed, sum up the essential differences. These differences considered with the conventions of late baroque music are the surest basis for developing a stylish approach towards performing Bach and his contemporaries. By 'style' it is not implied that a theoretical understanding of ornamentation and phrasing can in itself produce an authentic performance, for there was as much difference of opinion amongst eighteenth-century musicians as today about the niceties of interpretation. The decisive factor, as in all artistic matters, is in achieving the *spirit* of the style through the letter. Extemporization was an intrinsic part of a musician's skill; so much so, that musical graphics left almost everything regarding style to the instrumentalist, who would know automatically whether a piece was to be interpreted in the French or Italian manner, and how to embellish a line. In the eighteenth century it was just as impossible for the nuances of rhythm to be written out as it is in jazz today.

Tone Quality

The most important aspect to establish is the tone quality of the baroque oboe. We have many sources of information which do, in fact, vary considerably in their observations of distinguished players in the eighteenth century. Unfortunately, many music historians on the subject have frequently misjudged the tone of the old instruments either through lack of investigation, or simply by the perpetuation of commonly believed myths. Josef Marx quotes a number of these misconceptions including an item from the Harvard Dictionary of Music: '. . . the oboes of the eighteenth century and early nineteenth century were much more strident and piercing than the modern instrument, which is even more true of the still earlier instrument.' So much for unqualified evidence! It seems that such a notion of the early oboe was based not on the masterpieces by Hotteterre, but on the outdoor shawms which were played throughout the seventeenth century. An obsolescent period may well have spanned decades before the abandonment of the shawms in concerts and ceremonial music took place. Even Praetorius, writing about shawms in 1615, thought that the discant Schalmey sounded like the screeching of geese. But by 1671 we can be sure that the oboe had changed from an ugly duckling into a silver swan. By 1695 Bannister was able to describe its true tone quality in 'The Sprightly Companion' as 'brave and sprightly . . . For all that play upon this instrument to a reasonable perfection know, that with a good reed it goes as easie and soft as the Flute'. Mattheson describes it in 1713, when Handel was writing magnificent Sonatas and Concerti for the instrument: 'The oboe, next to the German flute, resembles most the human voice, when it is artfully played and handled like the voice . . .' What better description do we need to approach the slow movements of Handel's works or indeed the obbligati of Bach's arias?

The relationship with the violin is an extremely important area of consideration. In the concerti grossi and the oratorios of the late baroque, for much of the time the oboes double the strings to add lustre and clarity. One might suspect that Beethoven had G. C. Fischer's remarks in mind when he wrote the oboe solos in the Violin Concerto: 'The right tone of the Hoboy should be even and clear, from the lowest note to the highest, and not unlike the fine tone produced by the ablest Bow from the Violin . . .' Considering also the remarks of the rather effete Raguenet in 1702, the relationship seems to have been evident from the start: '. . . besides all the instruments that are common to us as well as the Italians, we have the hautboys, which, by their sounds, equally mellow and piercing, have infinitely the advantage of the violins in the brisk, lively airs . . .'

Henry Purcell

Some, if not all these observations may provide courage in approaching the first ravishing solos we come across in Henry Purcell during the 1690s.

Purcell's 'Come ye Sons of Art' has survived in a MS copy of 1765 by Robert Pinder (plate 14). Like all Purcell's works very little ornamentation is required; most embellishments are written out in full as in sixteenth-century melismata. At bars 12–13 it is stylish to insert a trill on the first note of the following figures: ♪♫ . This requires the first note (with the trill) to be dotted, and the short ornamental demi-semiquavers to become hemi-demi-semiquavers. The performance of any seventeenth- or eighteenth-century work demands of the oboist a nose for his own editing. Some editions of this work disclose glaring errors in the realization of the continuo part, usually relating to mannered diatonic nuances and a fussy interference with the very soloistic and elaborately composed duet for the voice and oboe. It is wise to keep Purcell's modal affinities in mind when considering tonal relationships in ornamentations.

Giving contemporary descriptions of tone is perhaps not so helpful as an actual performance on authentic instruments. Many recordings exist today which help us to move nearer to a true concept of the sound (see Appendix 4). But so far the problem of matching quality of performance with the substance of commentaries describing the music has not been solved. Too often we hear too wide a *vibrato* to match the kind of string sound which Purcell would have expected to hear. The violin was still a new instrument and only just becoming respectable enough to be played by 'gentlemen' who, for the most part, 'esteemed a Violin to be an instrument only belonging to a common Fidler'. *Vibrato* was by no means a fundamental aspect of its tone at this stage. Therefore, an oboe tone based on the 'smokescreen' of a wide *vibrato* would have been abhorrent to baroque musicians. The eighteenth-century instrument is easily susceptible to a wildness of pitch if played with the loose embouchure used by twentieth-century oboists or with an unsuitable reed. Add to this the characteristics of vocal sound in the baroque era and yet another aspect of style in sound is presented. Purcell was a male alto singer, and a fine one according to descriptions. *Vibrato* in such a falsetto register is unthinkable. It is this purity of tone which baroque musicians nurtured so carefully, no matter what other characteristics a piece demanded. The vibrancy of the boxwood oboe demands much more taming when played than the thicker, denser wood of modern instruments. For this reason it is more difficult for the modern player to achieve a lucid *piano* on the baroque oboe. There is a tendency to give up too much tone quality for the sake of easy production. The problem may arise from the inevitable reaction of the modern player to shy from biting on the reed for overblowing. As with the modern oboe, the reed is the decisive factor in obtaining the best results. The first consideration here is that the wider bore of the boxwood instrument needs a broader, 'fishtail' shaped reed; variable proportions are required for individual models, but it should be a triangular shape approximating $\frac{3}{8}$in on each side. This proportion provides for the wildness of intonation which the small, but heavily-cut fingerholes induce, and the firmness of embouchure required for pitch control in the cross and fork-fingering permutations and overblowing for the upper octave.

Fingering charts for these instruments is an area outside the scope of this book. This information is amply documented in Baines and Bate. Our main concern with the 18th century is to form a concept of performance which will take into account the essential nature of the baroque oboe while presenting the music written for it as faithfully as possible on a modern instrument.

101

Modern Editions

Composers and instrumentalists were prolific in writing about the interpretation of their own and others' music. Couperin's prefaces, Quantz's book 'On Playing the Flute', Hotteterre on the Flute, Recorder and Oboe, C. P. E. Bach on the art of keyboard performance – these are among the better-known writers we can draw on for information, but not, it must be stressed, for a clear-cut road to authenticity. There is, in fact, a great danger in becoming bogged down by the contradictions and constantly shifting idiosyncrasies which invade all the writings. It is the temperament of the substance we must aim to search out. Here there is yet another obstacle:

Oboists can only be rivalled by flautists in having to suffer the vast number of abortive editions of 18th-century music that invade the market today. Indeed, it is true to say that with few exceptions the quest for Urtext editions which have not been distorted by ruthless, inept editors has to lead to the libraries, either for first editions or, in the case of Bach and Handel, for the unspoiled Gesellschaft editions of the nineteenth century. An editor who realizes the figured bass, adds phrase marks, dynamics and other nuances without making it clear which is editorial and which original, does the greatest disservice to music.

These editions are under copyright protection and cannot be quoted here. As in the case of a particular Telemann sonata, they may be edited with the qualification of being 'revised, corrected and adapted' as an oboe sonata.

Adaptation is a perfectly valid form of realization; players of Telemann's times would certainly play several different instruments and adapt whatever piece they liked to whatever instrument they chose. Common practice. What is drastically misleading and unacceptable is a revision which, in this instance, misguides the performer into believing that the 'corrections' of the notation reproduce Telemann's intentions for the performance of a French 'Ouverture'.

The figured-bass realization (by yet another editor) demonstrates not only a profound ignorance of elementary harmony principles in his chord structures, but an agreement with the oboe editor on the interpretation of the faulty French Ouverture semiquavers of the oboe part. Presumably the task of revising, correcting and adapting is to give an edition of the original music in modern notation. Done without an understanding of the conventions governing eighteenth-century performances, such editions can do untold harm.

Perhaps the worst of editors are those who embellish a solo part without making it clear which is elaboration and which original. This is especially problematic, because embellishment is essentially extempore; i.e. it should sound as if the player is inventing the music on the spot. A good performer of eighteenth-century music can embellish a solo line in several different ways to the point where each performance has a different realization. Once written down, the graces and rhapsodic flourishes lose all sense of improvisation and inventive panache. Extemporization was a fundamental part of all good musicians' capabilities in the eighteenth century; it was this inventiveness which made music-making a constantly refreshing experience to listeners and performers alike.

In his History (1777) Burney describes a visit to C. P. E. Bach and how he spent a whole evening listening to the master extemporizing, emphasising the 'passion' of his playing. 'Passion' can be explained in twentieth century terms as vivid expression. It explains the true nature of eighteenth-century musical art in the gracing and embellishing of musical material. The quest for a stylish approach must be made with a sympathy for this spirit.

Style

When the oboe had fully emerged in the eighteenth century, European music was drawing on three quite distinctive styles: French, Italian and German. There was no sharp division in the use of these styles by composers of all countries, who could use all three within the course of a single piece. The French and Italian were utterly distinctive and required precise rendering on the part of the performer. The German style drew no sharp distinction between the other two, but was mainly based on the school of Lully between 1650–1700. The French, however, posed many special characteristics which demand acute awareness on the part of the oboist.

It is fairly easy to distinguish a French-style piece from an Italian if the editor has not played tricks by changing the language of a title, for a movement with a French tempo indication would call for appropriate French treatment. The most common forms are Suites, Dances with French titles and Overtures. Rhythmic alteration (pointing) affects the form of articulation which period players used. A true understanding of this form of phrasing is important in any interpretation, even if today we may dispense with an exact realization of the tonguing characteristics. Couperin explains this with an explanation of 'inequality' (*inégale*): 'We always make the first of each pair a little longer than the second. This inequality should be more pronounced in a gay piece than a sad one.' Movements in common time with a pulse of two in a bar, and all triple time movements may be treated *inégale*. More succinctly we may say that all time signatures can treat the notes of shortest value in three different ways:

1. They can be played as written – equal. If they are otherwise appropriate for inequality, that is step-wise intervals, the danger of misunderstanding is covered by the use of words such as '*détaché*', '*également*' and the like. With trustworthy editions these passages are accompanied by dots above the notes, a feature which did not imply *staccato* at this time.

2. Referring to Couperin's words above: the first note of each pair retains more value than the second. This does not mean that the rhythm was ♩. ♪ ; it was more like something between ♩♫. and ♩³♪ . This was described as *lourer* and applied to passages which moved step-wise. It could apply to the shortest notes in any passage if the tempo permitted. Robert Donington describes this effect very aptly as a 'lilting rhythm'; he should be referred to for a more comprehensive explanation of inequality.

3. When the first of two notes has a dot, the first note should be very much lengthened. This is called *pointer*. To clarify further, the following figurations should always be played equally: repeated notes; disjunct notes; more than two notes at a time that are slurred (C. P. E. Bach points out that a slur over dots on two groups means 'even', not '*staccato*':  notes mixed with shorter notes.)

The *lourer* characteristic is complemented by the form of articulation which players like Hotteterre suggest. In his Tutor he recommends that the tongue stroke be varied, 'to render playing more agreeable, and to avoid too much uniformity.' He recommends *tu* and *ru* as principal forms, and although inappropriate for the present-day oboist, it is nevertheless, very important to consider what this implies in the phrasing of the music. Generally, *tu* is used for strong beats and *ru* for lighter notes, providing a relationship of *-u* to emphasize phrasing punctuation.

Example 20

J. S. Bach *Suite No.4*

tu-ru tu tu   tu   tu-ru tu-ru tu   tu tu   tu tu

In example 20 (J. S. Bach, Suite No 4), *tu* is used almost exclusively on 𝅝 𝅗𝅥 𝅘𝅥 and on most quavers. Example 20 demonstrates that *ru* is usually intermixed with *tu* in passages of mixed-value notation.

Quantz demonstrates this concept with an example of *inégale* music using *ti* and *ri*, which means very much the same as Hotteterre's syllables:

Example 21

ti - ti ri ti ri ti ri ti ri

Quantz, *Guide to the Flute*, page 77 figure 10

105

More examples can be found in these treatises along with other variables. The point which must be established here is that tonguing, phrasing and all aspects of articulation were closely allied to the concept of bowing related to various note-values. Using these articulations for examples 20 and 21 gives the phrasing an almost inevitable *inégale*, and a bite and spring that are vital to the spirit of the music. A final example of how *tu-ru* or *ti-ri* demonstrate an inbuilt acknowledgement of this phrasing is shown to even better advantage in the Bach Orchestral Suite in C. The pairs of quavers in example 22 are written with slurs in modern practical editions, but in fact we ought to be thinking of *ti-ri* (or *tu-ru*) to achieve that essential 'lilt'.

Example 22

tu   tu-ru tu-ru tu   tu   tu   tu-ru tu-ru tu-ru

J. S. Bach: Suite No. 1 in C

The Suite is the form most popularly derived from the French school of Lully. Perhaps the most important point of style rests on the character of the dances from which all the movements derive their rhythmic structure. On this aspect of French style most contemporaries of Couperin emphasize the desirability of stresses (not accents) on the strong beats of the bar. The appoggiaturas in example 20 demonstrate this characteristic as a compositional feature of the dance associated with it. This kind of gentle emphasis of strong beats adds tremendous poise to the Gavotte and Bourrée, especially if one bears in mind that Couperin required string-players to use a down-bow on the first beat of each bar.

Generally the performer has always had a certain amount of freedom in the implementation of rhythmic alteration. One must avoid ultra-affectation or forcing it to the point of mannerism in movements that are fast and light. Alteration is essentially for rhythmic poise, a quality which is more obviously apparent when the *lourer* element is inverted to form a Scotch snap or *couler*. In authentic editions this is most commonly phrased as : ♪♪ ♪♪ and indicates a shortening of the first note sounding thus: *and* ♪.♪ ♪.♪.

More often than not it is written out in actual values. Considered with the aspects of poise described above it is of profound importance in playing Purcell (see **plate 14**).

Ornaments

Robert Donington provides an index for general reference which can help solve most anomalies. However, the oboist needs to exercise great care in the choice of graces for embellishment. For instance, the sign $+$ can have several interpretations, some of which will only be appropriate for the keyboard. The oboist can take this to mean a trill or an appoggiatura. All writers agree that these two are the most often used and most important of all graces in the French style.

The trill (*tremblement*) started on the upper note and had no turn at the end. It was never used on opening notes nor on notes approached by leap. Descending passages may be elaborated with them.

There were two main kinds of appoggiatura:

1. *Port-de-voix*, which Hotteterre describes as 'a tongue-stroke, anticipating the note on which you want to do it by a step from below', i.e. an ascending appoggiatura (example 23):

Example 23

Hotteterre, *Principles*

2. The *coulement*, which is a passing *appoggiatura*. Quantz describes it as played short and before the beat in a passage of descending thirds (example 24).

Example 24

Hotteterre, *Principles*

This is a very broad field for study and deserves further reading for the satisfaction of the complete oboist. But Quantz provides a good rule which gives the clue to treating *appoggiaturas* in the French style, with the dangerously encouraging remark that '*appoggiaturas* may be used even if not indicated. It is not enough to be able to play the different types of *appoggiaturas* with their proper values when they are marked. You must also know how to add them at the appropriate place when they are not indicated.' The following rule is given: 'If a long note follows one or more short notes on the down-beat or upbeat, and remains in a consonant harmony, an *appoggiatura* may be placed before the long note, in order to constantly maintain the agreeability of the melody. The preceding note will show whether it must be taken from above or below.'

The example he provides to illustrate this is a master-piece of compression (example 25).

Example 25

Quantz, *Guide to the Flute*

Embellishments deriving from the appoggiatura are important – the half-shake (a single mordent), example 26(a); the *pincé* (mordent), example 26(b); and the *doublé* (turn), example 26(c).

Example 26

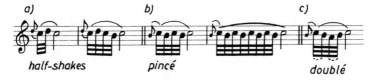

half-shakes   pincé   doublé

Quantz, *Guide to the Flute*

David Lasocki emphasizes Hotteterre's care in showing that the turn need not be completely slurred, that is, the *a′* followed by *b′* in example 26(c) may be tongued.

A beautiful grace is achieved with the '*accent*'. This is a sound which is borrowed from the ends of notes 'in order to give them more expression.' It is a very vocal characteristic which shows how a singing quality is innate to gracing.

Example 27

accent   accent

tu   tu tu   tu   tu tu

Hotteterre (op. cit.)

The sign ′ often replaces the small crotchet.

A clue to early 18th-century attitudes to *vibrato* as a grace can be found in the *flattement*. This was a *finger-vibrato* on the flat side of the note. Quantz relates it to the '*messa di voce*', a note held for a whole bar with crescendo and diminuendo, finishing with a turn.

The *battement* is an inverted mordent.

The twentieth century has shown a renewed interest in such extensions of expressive possibilities using cross-fingering techniques. Variable colours and 'bending' of a note were an everyday aspect of French performances from the first days of the oboe. Fingering tablatures in most of the tutors already mentioned show different cross-fingerings for enharmonic differences of intonation: e.g. F♯ and G♭.

There are many nuances of variation in interpreting the *appoggiatura*, but we have enough statements regarding an approach towards a French classification to satisfy our assurance over certain fundamentals. 'Hold the *appoggiatura* half the length of the main note', Quantz tells us; but if it embellishes 'a dotted note, that note is divided into three parts, of which the *appoggiatura* takes two . . .'. C. P. E. Bach tells us the same thing: 'The general rule for the length of the *appoggiatura* is to take from the following note, if duple, half its length; and if triple ⅔rds of its length'. Example 28 exemplifies this point. Some practical editions of the Bach Orchestral Suites defy this recommendation and advise that the *appoggiaturas* in the Bourrée II of Suite No. 4 should be played as quavers. This is even more untenable when we consider the emphasis C. P. E. Bach places on playing the *appoggiatura* louder than the main note.

Example 28

J. S. Bach: Suite No. 4

Fear of tautology or repetition of the same figuration can be overcome in this movement if the tempo is considered in the light of contemporary opinion. Donington quotes Talbot: 'Borée (one of five) French Measures of a very quick and rapid Movement.' Then Masson: 'Boree and Rigaudon, quicker (than Gavotte).' Quantz: 'Bourrée and Rigaudon played gayly and with a short light bow-stroke. Each bar has one beat of the (human) pulse.' Further evidence would show that a Bourrée in the French style would have been performed at a very rapid tempo, quite in keeping with J. S. Bach's own quoted penchant for lively tempi – and how marvellous to hear the magnificent trumpets setting the nobler tempo of the following Gavotte in elegant 'pointing' on the quavers!

It is a paradox that orchestras which happily play a Handel Bourrée with brilliant zest will approach the Bach movements, written in exactly the same style, at almost half speed.

A final point on Bach's Bourrée movements. Number II of Suite No. 1 in C uses the *slide* as an ornament. If we can take the same composer's Goldberg Variations as a guide in this matter (a work using the whole gamut of stylistic characteristics) the grace notes should be played on the beat, slightly accenting the first note. The spritely tempo the writer would favour would also make this interpretation more practicable as well as graceful.

There is an element of natural selection governing the laws of musical heredity. We need to feel our realizations of works as a search for the root of the composition whether through written evidence or information engendered by association. I remember with conviction the moment I first desired to hear Handel's Pastoral Symphony from 'Messiah' played on wind instead of strings. Others have worked on the same hunch, producing performances which sound much more convincing than the slow and rather tedious realization on strings. The movement is called 'Piffa', derived from the Italian bagpipe player, *'piffero'*. A Christmas spent in Rome gave me the opportunity of hearing some traditional music played by Neapolitan *pifferari*. The tune they often played convinced me of Handel's real intentions for this movement (see example 29a). It is well within the bounds of possibility that this was the self-same tune that Handel heard during his Christmas stay in Rome in 1709. A comparison with example 29b may add some confidence to this assumption.

Example 29a

Handel *Piffa*

Whatever the case, there is no doubt about the association of the two examples to Neapolitan *piffero* traditions. A convincing realization of the Pastoral Symphony may benefit from some awareness of the tempo indication in example 29a.

Having found our way to Italy the road to discovery is less difficult to follow, for here notation in the seventeenth and eighteenth centuries generally means what it says. There is none of the mannerism, subtlety or restraint which colours the French Baroque. The main fields of characterization are in the very elaborate gracing of the Adagios and the manner of dotted rhythms. Paradoxically the Italian style is more important for the oboist than the French because most of the forms which include the instrument as an orchestral part, or as a soloist, are Italian. Sonata, Concerto, Sinfonia, Air, Gigue, Minuet are the most significant. The Oratorio, Opera and Cantata all draw on these forms.

Much more emphasis was placed on melody than on figurative invention. The training of all instrumentalists equipped them with a sure knowledge of Harmony and Counterpoint which was absolutely essential for the skills of improvisation required for elaborating material and extemporizing in cadenzas. The notes of a slow Adagio or an Aria were often little more than a framework for the instrumentalist to weave elaborate inventions of musical tracery. There was a long tradition of improvisation in Italy from the earliest days of divisions (melodic embellishments) practised by the viol consorts. Before examining these techniques let us touch on some aspects of style where the Italians and the French are parallel.

'Double-dot, please!' This glib cliché of twentieth-century rehearsal rooms is often the conductor's augury for a garbled performance of eighteenth-century music, no matter how well-intentioned the instruction may be. The truth is that dots which require lengthening vary in the proportion of duration according to the context. So a correct response to the conductor might well be made earnestly: 'Yes, but *how* double-dotted?' The quality of the dot, like all aspects of rhythmic deviation in eighteenth-century music, is to emphasize the prevailing character (mood, if you like) of the movement. Wherever dots need to give more value to a note it is generally to provide more spring on the short notes, more poignancy (as in the Purcell, **plate 14**), more robustness, or more gravity. The dot simply varies its length according to the mood expressed. Quantz provides a valuable table of reference for this concept (example 30):

Example 30

He explains that the aim is to sustain 'the animation which these notes must express . . . The notes after the dots in (a) and (b) must be played just as short as those in (c) whether the tempo is slow or fast.' Relationships with dotted notes in another voice are explained with an example which gives the smallest note the same value in all cases (example 31):

Example 31

It is also suggested that lifting the dotted note adds crispness to the figuration. The duration of the shortest note of the movement dictates the duration of all notes following a dot. This is a very significant factor of all French Overtures whether by French, German or Italian composers. The Overture of Bach's Suite No. I (besides a suggestion of 'pointing'

on the semiquavers) should sound all dotted figures ♩⃫

as ♩⃫ , approximately, stopping the trill and the sound very briefly after the value of a quaver. The short note needs to be considered as belonging to the first note of the following beat and not to the one whose ligature it shares. Hotteterre's *tu-ru-tu* would clarify the point. Handel's G minor Oboe Concerto exemplifies this in the first movement. The predominant short-note value is a demi-semiquaver; the French and Italians would agree with the rule that all the notes after dots take the value of this, the shortest note. There are no phrase-marks or dynamics in the original until bars 9, 10 and 12, where Handel has been careful to ensure that two-note groups should be slurred. This is a 'Grave' movement and does not necessarily need ornamentation; in which case the opening section for the oboe at bar 6 sustains a noble character with very dotted notes (example 32):

Example 32

tu   tu ru tu   tu ru tu   ru tu ru tu ru tu   tu

It is a powerful statement which can be enhanced by a short break before the articulation of each short note, the B♭ in the first bar becoming a demi-semiquaver, and the trill stopping on the dot with the pair of demi-semiquavers becoming something like hemi-demi-semiquavers and tongued with *ru-tu* in mind. C. P. E. Bach would ask us to begin the trill on the upper note because it is preceded by the same note.

The second movement of this work provides an opportunity for the indulgence of a twentieth-century oboist's fetish – that is, slurring two and tonguing two in groups of running semiquavers. In this instance it would be much more tasteful to slur them in groups of four to provide a definitive character to the phrasing. The expedient of the fetish described above will always sound contrived because it side-steps the real solution to a problem of technical facility.

The Bach Orchestral Suites are prodigious in feats of oboistic display, providing other examples of rhythmic alteration relevant to all styles. The *Ouverture* of Suite No. 4 in D is a good example for another general rule which clarifies the often blurred distinction between compound and duple metre in baroque music. The rule is simple enough: 'assimilate all dotted rhythms to the dominant rhythm of the movement, no matter what the time signature may be.'

Example 33(a)

Example 33(b)

Some practical editions make no concession to editorial distortion in the phrasing of this work. Where Bach has been careful to relate all phrase marks to the rhythmic and harmonic structure of each phrase, these editors have simply ironed-out everything by slurring all the triplet groups without variation. From a practical point of view

would be unwieldy on a baroque oboe, because of the awkward slur from the overblown *b″* down to c″♯. Nor would it be particularly graceful on a violin. Bach requires

Throughout the movement the repeated note figuration (e.g. the first oboe part in example 33) consistently requires both notes to be tongued because this is the distinctive motiv of the whole movement, providing a beautifully poised rhythmic grace. In a *Gigue*, such as the last movement of Suite No. 3, the character is quite different from the French overture of No. 4, and faster. Here the slurring of each three-note group is essential for the strings, and appropriate on the oboes. On this point the Bach-Gesellschaft edition is wholly consistent with the concepts of articulation explained by Hotteterre and Quantz. The latter is explicit here: 'Slurred notes must be played as they are indicated, since a particular expression is often sought through them'.

These graphic conventions were hard to die and could still be discerned as late as the 1840s in Chopin (example 34).

Example 34

Chopin *Fantasy - Impromptu in C sharp minor*

Nor indeed is the nature of *rubato* dissimilar between the two centuries. In 1717 Couperin instructs us: 'Preludes should be played freely and *with plenty of rubato*, except when the word "mesuré" occurs . . .' Example 34 can be interpreted either as written or as a triplet in the right hand fourth beat in the manner of the Bach Suites discussed. However, Couperin leaves room for an alternative when he tells us: 'The suspension – a note played late – corresponds to a crescendo on a stringed instrument, and is scarcely used except in slow and tender pieces' – which could, of course, equally apply to the Chopin example. A similiar connection between the centuries arises in the manner of playing trills. 'Shakes' writes Couperin, 'must always begin on the upper note, and they must grow faster towards the end . . .'

Handel's G minor Concerto demonstrates the need for lengthening the dot in Grave movements. This characteristic is even more emphasized in purely Italian movements such as the Siciliana in the same composer's B♭ Concerto (see example 35). This convention was also longstanding.

Example 35

Siciliano

Handel Concerto in B♭

Handel provides no dynamics and no phrasing. The performer simply has to rely on an examination of the conventions. In this instance there is more than a hint of the French '*accent*' discussed above, the very short semiquavers providing a beautiful lilt and an expressive, song-like line to the repeated notes in each triplet group throughout the movement. The dotted phrase-mark in example 35 indicates this manner.

The Siciliana is either 6/8, as in Handel's B♭ Concerto, or 12/8, like the first movement of Telemann's Sonata in A minor. Phrasing manners are identical. But it would please Quantz to hear figurations like ♩. ♫♩ in the Telemann movement with dots played as long as possible: 'The longer the dots . . . are held . . . the more flattering and pleasing are notes of this kind.' The lyrical oboe obbligato in Handel's aria 'Love in her Eyes Sits Playing', from 'Acis and Galatea', finds extra grace from this advice. Marches, too, should share the 'long dot' and 'crisp short notes', characteristic of the Grave and Siciliana movements.

Extemporization and Embellishment

Any relationship with French attitudes vanishes in the Adagios of Italian Concertos and Sonatas. This is where the eighteenth-century musician became an extempore virtuoso, and in some instances showed the composer what could be done with the means available. A good instrumentalist would never dream of performing the same embellishments in successive performances. The range of extempore possibilities is touched on in Donington, who provides a chart of possibilities for one melody by Tartini. There are no fewer than seventeen variations – and the changes could go on ringing for many more examples. Oboists, more than any other wind-players, should take pride in the adulation that followed great performers of the eighteenth century. Even the hard-to-please Handel is on record as a great admirer of the instrument. The Six Sonatas for two oboes were composed, like most of the chamber music, when Handel was young; in this case when he was in his eleventh year. Many years after their composition these sonatas were brought to England by Lord Polworth, who presented them to his teacher, the flautist Weidemann. When they were finally shown to Handel he laughed and said, 'I used to write like the Devil in those days, but chiefly for the hautbois, which was my favourite instrument'. How lucky we are! The two most monumental musicians of the age discovered some of their highest achievements through the oboe.

The importance of harmonic motivation in ornamentation cannot be stressed strongly enough in Italian music. Quantz again is the arbiter of taste on this matter: '[It is mere bad taste] to load the Adagio with a quantity of ornamentation, and to disguise it in such a way that often among ten notes there is scarcely one which is in harmony with the fundamental part, and the principal melody of the piece can hardly be heard any longer.' In other words, whatever notes you choose for the embellishments they must make good constructive harmonic sense. The implied harmony of the melodic line is the true structure for embellishment. Quantz indicates that even in the eighteenth century the study of harmony and counterpoint was sometimes considered by students to be an academic chore, and separates the wheat from the chaff in unminced words: 'There are even some professional musicians who, lacking the necessary feeling and insight, are gratified to see the end of the Adagio arrive. Yet a true musician may distinguish himself by the manner in which he plays the Adagio . . .' In discussing the subject it must be remembered that writing down graces and embellishments cannot provide the whole truth of the matter. Written symbols are the theory of embellishment, which can only take wing when emancipated from the page and allied to the 'passion' of an involuntary response in performance to a well-learned vocabulary. 'That which does not come from the heart does not easily reach the heart'. This vocabulary is clearly set out in the books mentioned by Quantz and C. P. E. Bach.

The following pages discuss the most important procedures these famous essays recommend. The French characteristics which have been briefly explained must, according to Quantz, be assimilated as the basic ingredients of ornamentation before the more lengthy embellishments of the Italian style can be approached.

Handel's Sonata in C minor (No. VIII in Chrysander) is especially interesting as a model, for it has two Grave movements, the first and third. To follow the eighteenth-century writers' recommendations it is essential to use a copy which follows the basic format of the first edition – e.g. Chrysander. This simply provides two lines of music on each stave. The upper line carries the solo part which contains nothing more than the notes themselves – no nuances. The lower line carries the figured bass continuo. If the soloist cannot see the bassline or does not know it from memory, the task of ornamenting is impossible. The embellishments can only be successful if the harmony is understood.

The paucity of material presented to the performer signifies the great importance attached to embellishment and extemporization. Phrasing marks would be inhibiting to a free interpretation of the music. The substance of a piece was in its form, and the performer's artistry was demonstrated by his skill in conveying this insight through the perfection of his elaboration. It is a consistent characteristic of the winding tracery of baroque architecture and art, reflected in music by a superstructure of intricate embellishment.

Handel *Sonata in C Minor*
(1st movt.)

Example 36

121

Movement I of Handel's C minor Sonata (example 36) incorporates most of the common graces and extempore embellishments of single notes. The long note which begins the piece may be treated as a '*messa di voce*' (*crescendo-diminuendo*), or simply as a *crescendo* beginning from the smallest sound possible. Although dynamic degrees were only written as *p* or *f*, the use of the *messa di voce*, along with gradations of tone within a phrase, were essential to expression and phrasing ('passion'). The concept of terraced dynamics is, on the whole, a 20th-century myth. Neither too much nor too little is the consensus of opinion among eighteenth-century writers. Handel's first phrase is designed to encourage the growth of tone from the beginning, rising on the progressive bass to fulfilment at the return of the tonic chord on the third beat of the second bar. The writer's added graces complement this approach, giving extra poignancy to the following *diminuendo* with a turn; although it must be added that only an *appoggiatura* would be tasteful if the third and fourth beats shared the same chord. But the harmony progresses and the turn gives the changed relationship of the E♭ in both chords extra significance. The general rule is followed throughout regarding *appoggiaturas*, which must always be tongued, that is, never slurred from the preceding note.

Bar 5 shows the flower of the movement opening on another *messa di voce* (⟨ ⟩) in the relative major. This blossoming can be enhanced by extempore embellishments on the continuo harmony. The harpsichordist has an excellent opportunity to set the figurations in bars 4 and 5 which would be the cue for the oboist to imitate and reflect on the mood created. Bar 6 shows a mordent in the third beat. All trills shown follow the same rule: they are introduced by an *appoggiatura* and finish with a turn (Quantz). Bar 15 is the first example of a '*battement*' or inverted mordent. Bars 7 and 8 present wonderful opportunities for intuitive response between the three-note phrase of the bass and the oboe. The vaguest hint of a cadenza (just coming into fashion in Handel's youth) is suggested in the last two movements. In this instance it would be ungracious to do more than a florid extemporization with no significant change of time.

The second movement, Allegro, is amazingly characteristic of the mature Handel, demonstrating a truly inventive command of the language. It is a fughetta. After the solo presentation of the subject by the oboe, the continuo answers in direct imitation of the oboe's counter-subject – but at the opposite end of the bar! The oboist may set the characterization of the subject which the continuo must imitate. Ideally, the semiquavers of example 37 (bars 9–12 of Handel C minor II) should be tongued lightly with a very gentle articulation in a semi-*legato* manner. Chapter 4 explains this in more detail; *tu-ru* would suit the 18th-century player more appropriately. Slurring a few of these semiquavers can add form to the phrase if, for instance, the bracketed figurations of example 37 are phrased in relief to emphasize the shift of accent between the bars. Bach and Handel wove intriguing shifts of rhythmic emphasis in much of their music. Conveying this aspect is an important part of interpreting the works.

Example 37

Handel *Sonata in C Minor*
(2nd movt., bars 9–12)

Example 38 Adagio

126

Example 38 (Handel C minor III) is a written-out realization of the characteristics which combined French ornaments with Italian extempore procedures in the performance of the Adagio. It is the moment for the oboist either to blossom or to flounder as an artist.

This realization follows the melodic line throughout, at first with simple triplet figures interspersed with ornaments. Trills that sound as fast as electric bells should be avoided. Many of these short French ornaments are related to faster movements. When used with the Adagio extempore phrases, they should adopt the character of the movement to sound more relaxed and melodic. This particularly applies to trills and turns (bars 1 and 3 respectively). C. P. E. Bach's stressed *appoggiatura* takes a very natural place in bar 4. For the rest, the procedures are very closely woven to the melodic line, and move in a linear manner to enhance the shifting harmony of bars 13–16, and to colour the poignancy of bars 16–20 in the relative minor with a dark *pianissimo*. Repeating the same motiv in the tonic at bar 21 is a dramatic moment, coloured by a restless descent to the subdominant in the next bar; dramatic, because the embellishment here is overladen with clinging *appoggiaturas*, which can be quite operatic in gesture. The *appoggiatura* in bar 26, although not written out in the oboe part as such, is positively implied by the 4/3 suspension of the continuo bass on the second beat – a procedure which demonstrates how much the *appoggiatura* was taken for granted as an embellishment.

The last three bars constitute a compression of elaboration in the form of a short cadenza. Although the French abstained from any hint of such an insertion, Italian composers made a feature of it, often suffering profoundly as a result. Their performers took astonishing liberties with this moment in the piece, so much so that composers eventually included a moving bass throughout the closing bars to safeguard the music from such barbaric attitudes. This tells us that restraint should be shown, and that the pulse of the movement should not always be changed. Example 38 is a case where the absence of a pause in the penultimate bar denies any caden-

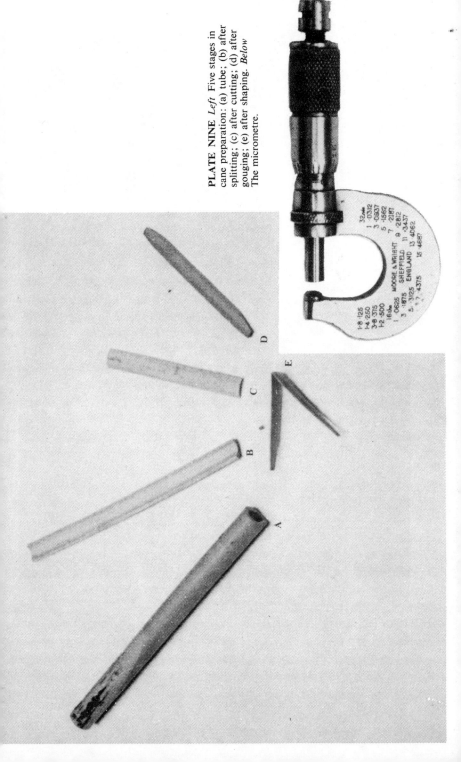

PLATE NINE *Left* Five stages in cane preparation: (a) tube; (b) after splitting; (c) after cutting; (d) after gouging; (e) after shaping. *Below* The micrometre.

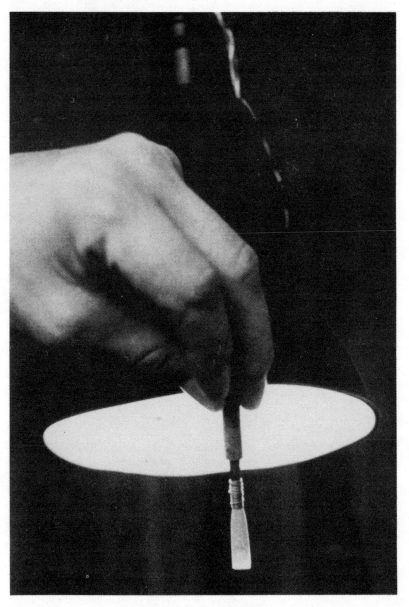

PLATE TEN *Above* The finished reed against the light.

PLATE ELEVEN *Opposite, above* The correct position for the reed on the lower lip. *Below* Sealed embouchure.

PLATE TWELVE Correct posture.

tial treatment that affects the continued pulse of the piece.

The fourth movement can adopt the advice of Quantz without further interpretation: 'In the Allegro . . . the plain air must be embellished and made more agreeable by *appoggiaturas*, and by the other little essential graces, as the *passion of the moment* demands.' My italics are intended to stress the essentially improvisatory aspect of embellishing. Example 39 provides a few ideas relating to the advice on which all the writers agree: that only the shorter French graces are operable in the Allegro, and then only the second time round. We are also advised to do repeats at *p* if the first statement is played *f*. This can be overdone to the point of mannerism, so it is suggested that within this field, phrasing nuance must allow for considerable variation of dynamic range.

A final word from Quantz regarding 'shakes' in the Allegro: 'If an instrumentalist . . . were to possess all the skills required by good taste in performance, and yet could not strike good shakes, the total art would be incomplete.' Chapter 4 discusses the techniques for acquiring 'good shakes'.

Quantz was writing at a time when the baroque era had reached its zenith. His own music can best be described as *galant*. Within a decade or two this style was to die almost as quickly as the obsolescent harpsichord.

C. P. E. Bach and Quantz were the giants of *galant* – those who self-consciously adopted all the mannerisms of the French and, infusing them into melody rather than counterpoint, created a bridge to the world adopted by Mozart. Such a transitional situation was bound to draw from the past while pointing to the future. At the height of this fashion dissertations poured from the pens of Quantz, C. P. E. Bach, Avison, Leopold Mozart and Geminiani almost within months of each other in the early 1750s. They form a magnificent assessment of musical practice from 1700–1750; but in some ways they also proclaim an obituary to the era.

Music history is often out of step with its contemporary literary fashions. Nowhere is this more pronounced than in the classical period from 1770–1800. In Europe this period was the crest of the romantic wave, when the political arena of

Handel *Sonata in C Minor*
(4th movt.)

Example 39

Allegro

the whole continent nurtured a new spirit of revolt. But in the Courts and concert rooms, the lace and grace of the rococo sustained musical activities and thoughts derived from the spirit that informed the Essays. By 1780 the relevance of the Essays was almost extinct. For the oboist the information they convey applies as much to J. S. Bach as to rococo practice. Therefore, it is to him we must return with the evidence of the Essays in mind.

The Brandenburg Concerti of Bach's early years take all this substance into account. All the Italian manners are here, but unlike most composers he prefers to write his ornaments and graces in full. Some good advice offered by Geminiani to string-players provides an interesting qualification for the manner of articulation the oboes should adopt in the Brandenburg Concerto No. 1: rapid semi-quavers 'are to be played plain and the Bow is not to be taken off the Strings'. Hotteterre's *tu-ru tu-ru* concurs with this approach. The bite and spring which bring Bach to life require this lucid articulation of the oboes more than any other feature.

The beautiful Adagio anticipates the style of the obbligati in the cantatas, prefacing much we may learn about embellishing such movements in other composers. Time values in this Adagio require special attention. Go to the Gesellschaft edition to discover that some modern editions have altered the time values in the second bar, and similar places throughout. Example 40 is correct.

Example 40

J. S. Bach *Brandenburg Concerto No.1*
(2nd mvt.)

Many of the problems relating to the performance of baroque music arise from the prolific output of composers, and the speed at which they had to work. Instrumentalists were fully aware of the responsibility this created for them but they were more widely trusted in their initiative than Couperin would normally allow. The First Orchestral Suite of Bach pleads for such common sense over the repeats. While these are essential to each piece it is unwise for the oboist to play all of them when unison sections occur. The oboes are rarely provided with a break throughout the work. Strings can carry the burden easily with one oboe from time to time. Thus: *Courante:* Both oboes first time. 2nd Oboe only in the first repeat. 1st Oboe only in the second repeat. The recapitulation requires both. *Gavotte I:* Solo throughout; divide the repeats between both players. This provides renewed vigour for *Gavotte II*, where no breaks can be made. *Forlane* and *Menuet I*, as written. *Menuet II* provides a natural break before the repeat of Menuet I. *Bourrée I:* for a relief from oboe colouring, as well as the need for a break, the repeats can be silent for the oboes. This also provides time to recover for *Bourrée II*, which is for Wind only. *Passepied I:* repeats divided between players. *Passepied II:* Tutti.

There is a special problem attached to the ethos of the eighteenth-century composer. Although he had to deal with a commercial industry in the same manner as twentieth-century composers, he had a more insistent problem of deadline. It was not simply a feat of dedication on Handel's part to produce 'Messiah' in three weeks. With a performance scheduled, there was no question of failing to do so. In lesser hands such a task frequently resulted in the production of a mechanical exercise. This 'sewing-machine' syndrome was simply the result of commercial pressure.

For this reason alone we have inherited an artistic problem today in having to reproduce what could only be conveyed by convention in the eighteenth century – a convention, moreover, which was often represented by shorthand methods. The fact that J. S. Bach did not leave so much to conjecture is an interesting feature of his genius, apart from the answers he provides to so many questions in the written-out realizations of his flute sonatas. No bowing to the fads of parodying soloists! Most of the humorous remarks of Quantz and C. P. E. Bach on performers attest to the appalling realizations the music often had to suffer as a result of skeletal techniques, as if such total reliance on the performer was in some way flattering, but not necessarily reflected in the realizations, as so many commentaries indicate. Shorthand methods made it possible for Telemann to compose forty operas, six hundred overtures in the French style, and hundreds of other works, while fulfilling the role of publisher and impresario in one lifetime.

The bare material of a baroque chamber work (again, as distinct from the finely-woven tracery of J. S. Bach) demanded profound dedication to its ephemeral intentions on the part of the performer. Observing some aspects of the commercial music industry of the twentieth century is to see the same 'sewing-machine' craft committed to the same process of dissipation. It eventually led the nineteenth-century composer to retreat into a subjective world of romantic fantasy in the glorification of fable. The eighteenth century failed to recognize its true masters such as J. S. Bach until this new spirit was launched by the Romantics.

If Couperin spent his entire life complaining that nobody understood him, it is simple proof that neumes can say nothing of the spiritual aspirations of music unless they can be formulated into a vernacular of commonly comprehendable language. This can only exist on a plane where spirit and letter become one in the performer.

Some of the conventions of baroque manner demonstrate laziness, even on the part of some of the period's finest composers. Yet J. S. Bach achieved clarity with hardly a written word on the subject. He was a law unto himself. Others were seduced by convention. For this reason it is good that they leave us a verbal record of their intentions. Without these treatises we would lose the life-line to the spirit and manner of baroque music.

Six
Playing Classical Music

> 'Signor Besozzi's messa di voce, or swell, is prodigious; indeed he continues to augment the force of a tone so much, and so long, that it is hardly possible not to fear for his lungs.'

It would be interesting to know which concerto Besozzi was playing when Charles Burney heard him. Judging from the quotation above he may well have been describing the cadenza, which gave so much freedom for the performer to demonstrate his *messa di voce*. The kind of oboe that produced such prodigious feats in the 1770s was classical. There were no outstanding differences between baroque and classical instruments. In Chapter 2 I pointed out that fundamentally, they were the same two– or three-keyed instruments which relied on fork-fingerings and embouchure manipulation for correct pitches of all the twelve semitones. The few changes that had been made since 1700 were simplifications of the baroque design. Ornament was reduced to a minimum around the sockets and baluster, while the keys were supported on the pivot wires by raised mountings on the wood. (See **plate 3.)**

Like composers, eighteenth-century performers were neither fêted (as the Greek aulists) nor esteemed as an élite (like twentieth-century soloists). Musicians were treated all of a kind, that is, as hired servants to be paid to do what was asked of them. The fact that a composition was of no financial value to a composer once it was written made the voluminous production of new music and its immediate performance a persistent responsibility for the instrumentalist.

Like Besozzi, most instrumentalists were also composers. The eighteenth century was teeming with such musicians. Mozart was one of the most ill-used of them all. These matters are well-illustrated in his letters. For instance, on the occasion of a proposed performance of a Sinfonia Concer-

tante* in Paris in 1778, the Director of the Concerts Spirituels, Le Gros, had taken responsibility for having the parts
prepared. The oboist Ramm was to play in the ensemble, and
demonstrated magnificent support for the composer, which
Mozart describes in a letter to his father. Having discovered
the score hidden away the composer questioned Le Gros: 'A
propos. Have you given the Sinfonia Concertante to be
copied?' 'No,' he replied, 'I forgot all about it.' Mozart continues: 'As of course, I would not command him to have it
copied and performed, I said nothing; but when I went to the
concert on the two days when it should have been performed,
Ramm and Punto came up to me in the greatest rage to ask
me why my Sinfonia Concertante was not being played. "I
really don't know", I replied. "It's the first I've heard of it. I
know nothing about it." Ramm flew into a passion and in the
music-room he cursed Le Gros in French, saying it was a
dirty trick and so forth. What annoys me most in the whole
affair is that Le Gros never said a word to me about it – I
alone was to be kept in the dark . . .' The composer Cambini
was probably behind this plot.

Mozart was accompanied by Ramm and three other colleagues from the great Mannheim orchestra on this Paris trip.
The letters demonstrate the high regard each had for the
other. These collaborations exerted a profound effect on
Mozart's writing for the instruments, especially the oboe.
'Ramm', writes Mozart, 'is a very good, jolly, honest fellow
of about 35 who has already travelled a great deal and con-
sequently has plenty of experience.' And, more amusingly:
'Ramm is a decent fellow, but a libertine.' The fine qualities
which inspired Mozart to compose the exquisite Quartet for
Oboe and Strings were described by F. J. Lipowsky in his
'Baierisches Musik-Lexikon' of 1811 and quoted by Alfred
Einstein:

'. . . it is not too much to say that no one has yet been able to
approach him in beauty, roundness, softness and trueness of tone
on the oboe, combined with the trumpet-like depth of his forte.
He plays, for the rest, with a delicacy, a lightness, and a power of

* Not the surviving K297^b, the origin of which is still shrouded in mystery.

expression that enchant the listener; he handles this instrument wisely, according to its true, individual nature, and with a practical skill possessed by few oboists; in an Adagio his interpretation is full of feeling, but he also knows how to express spirit, and fire, if the effect and the inspiration demand them.'

This is, of course, an invaluable document for us to discover the true nature of classical oboe sound: 'beauty, roundness, softness' are in accord with the natural response of the classical instrument when an appropriate reed is used; 'trueness' is very likely a qualification for good intonation. 'Delicacy . . . lightness . . . power of expression' – these are all terms which point to a feminine quality of sweetness, a quality which the nineteenth-century oboe, although slow to mature, finally achieved in the late Triébert and Lorée instruments. The somewhat narrower bore of the classical instrument compared to the baroque model would contribute towards such qualities. Unlike Einstein, I consider the 'trumpet-like depth of his forte' an excellent description of the lower notes in statement-like passages, especially when they are followed by wide-ranging leaps in a *forte* dynamic, as in examples 41 and 42:

Example 41

Example 42

This point must be considered in the light of Lipowsky's experience of trumpet sound in 1811, many years before the grand F trumpet of Berlioz' orchestra had evolved.

The Oboe Quartet was composed in 1781 at a very optimistic stage in Mozart's life, after the tremendous success of 'Idomeneo'. He felt more free to express himself without the shackles of his Salzburg service, to nurture the compulsion away from *galant* towards his mature contrapuntal style. We see this in many aspects of the Quartet. Consider the beginning of the development where the falling fourth motiv (an inversion of the first two notes of the piece) forms a contrapuntal web of rich sonority and harmonic elegance. This statement is characteristic of the whole piece in the convolutions of its phrase structure. *Galant* in simple terms could be described as 'tune and accompaniment'. Mozart rarely subscribed to this manner even in his very early compositions. There is always an abundant texture of variable figurative elements in each subject. This is intensely important to consider in approaching Mozart, because this constant awakening of new elements and motivs must be projected in performance and characterized with the 'spirit and fire' or 'power of expression' which Ramm's playing inspired in the Quartet. Example 43 exposes three motivs within one phrase:

Example 43

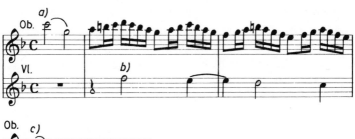

Mozart, Oboe Quartet

Each has an entirely different character: (a) is the noble figure which sustains the first part of the development; (b) is an extension of the second part of the subject:

and is set against the counter-subject in the violin, which the oboe takes up in an inversion of the two subjects in oboe and violin following the first statement. It is good, honest fugue technique which requires acknowledgement in the give and take of the performance. Finally (c) is a cadential motiv, smooth and contrasting. Each of these motivs needs distinctive characterization if the richness of the texture is to be realized. Nowhere in the piece does the oboe become dominant at the expense of the strings. We are constantly having to think of texture, not melody and accompaniment. The contrapuntal kaleidoscope must carry infinite shades of dynamic nuance within the ebb and flow of each motiv and phrase formation, very much in the manner which Lipowsky describes in Ramm's playing.

This aspect is intensified in the sublime minor slow movement, where the oboe begins with a ranging descant above the strings' sonorous motivs to transform into the melodic phrase of the first subject. The turn into a major key prepares the presentation of the passionate second subject *not* in the relative major, but in B♭ major. This kind of harmonic subtlety is perhaps the most distinguishing feature of both Mozart and Haydn, and one which performers must constantly recognize in their interpretations. The aim is to project this miraculous transformation with the intensity such restless shifting of harmony involves. The cadenza requires no more than a simple, poignant scale (it is a very short movement):

Example 44

Mozart, Oboe Quartet

The movement falls to a close with the gentle weeping of the second subject motiv.

Of all the joys an oboist can relish there is perhaps no other work to match this Quartet in the range of expression and virtuosity it indulges. There is bravura, sadness, delight, humour, joy . . . and all the time the oboist can 'sing' with rich sound and perfectly balanced phrases covering the whole range of the instrument. And now in the last movement the dance begins and we wing away on sweeping melodies and flashes of brilliant display. Mozart includes one of his most daring strokes at the point where the strings sustain the 6/8 of the dance while the oboe whirls off into cascades of semi-quavers in 4/4. The fourth bar of this section sometimes causes trouble:

Example 45

should sound as follows:

Example 46

It is cadenza-like and needs to be thrown off in a flourish.

The tempo of the movement must be judged exactly to achieve the brilliance required. One notch too slow and we have a very pedestrian waltz on our hands instead of the lithe, zestful rondo Mozart intends.

The Oboe Concerto ('Ramm's Warhorse' as Mozart describes it) is a more conventional work composed in 1777 for the Mannheim oboist, Ferlendis. The slow movement pinpoints a special problem in performance with the constant use of the high register which the soloist must project strongly through the orchestral texture. The thinner range a'' to c'' is constantly used. This register has less carrying power on the modern reed and oboe than the classical instrument.

It is here, more than anywhere in the repertoire, that considerations of abdominal support and a relaxed embouchure require the greatest assertion. One moment of tension is

139

enough to destroy the effect of serene indeed *sublime*, smoothness of *legato*. In Chapter 4 there is much discussion of finger action in *legato* playing. This slow movement is a good testcase for achieving the speed of movement required by the finger, using as little muscular activity as possible, so that for each change of note the fingers move quickly, but as late and minimally as possible. The separation of abdominal tension from all other relaxed muscular activity is vital here because slow sustained sound in this high register requires much air. Projection of air must be as restrained as possible while the abdominal 'push' provides the essential support for the air stream. Ultimately this is achieved by a sense of excitement in the lower area of the chest cavity. This sense of vitality can be described as what is loosely called 'musicianship' or 'expression'. It has no name, but may well be triggered into action in this movement with deep consideration of the technical facets mentioned above, and explained in detail in Chapter 4.

Inserting a Cadenza

The performer-composer of the eighteenth century had little or no problem in providing a display of virtuoso brilliance in the cadenza of a concerto because the language and idiom of the music he played was, more often than not, that of his own time. Two hundred or so years later we must accept the fact that our experience of music is coloured by the vast number of influences of the intervening years, which may well affect our manner of approach towards inventing a classical cadenza. The following points are offered as guidelines, and illustrated in examples 47–49.

Style is dictated by harmonic idiom, melodic intervals, and rhythmic figurations. Therefore, an approach must be made through pastiche, which can inculcate the clichés established by these principles. The concerto cadenza (unlike fantasia inventions, which are always written out) needs to sustain the time signature of the parent movement.

The harmonic implications of the 6/4 chord, presented by the orchestra as a spring-board for the soloist, remain throughout the cadenza. It is the starting point as well as the

Example 47

Cadenza (1st movt.)
Presto

Mozart *Concerto in C*

close. Any deviation of key on the way must ultimately return to this chord. What better reason can we have for keeping the cadenza short enough to sustain this cumulative effect?

There are too many unreliable editions available to ignore what may seem an obvious fact to many: the implied harmony of a single line of melody and figuration must be explicit. If there is no harmonic structure in a cadenza the result is ludicrous. Statements of thematic material from the movement can be balanced with episodes based on the composer's figurations in harmonic sequences. Variations of key and modulation stem from such episodes.

A restatement of the first subject in the tonic key at the outset is artistic suicide. The cadenza is what its title suggests – the close of a movement. Any suggestion of a new beginning, or indeed another recapitulation, is dramatically illogical and unimaginative.

Examples 47, 48 and 49 illustrate these recommendations:

Example 48

Example 49

Cadenza (3rd mvt.)
Allegro

All the figurative and melodic material is Mozart's. The harmonic structure and bravura episodes are also based on characteristic formulae of Mozart's style.

Classical Orchestral Technique

The constant expansion of the orchestral repertoire in the twentieth century presents the vision of a balloon of musical material becoming more and more inflated to the point of bursting. For an oboist who takes his job seriously (and I know of none who do not) this can be a menacing thought, if all aspects of idiom and style of interpretation are constantly demanded of him/her. However, the necessity to revise one's thinking in the light of new research and discovery is the life-blood of artistic vitality. The absence of such a vocational approach creates the danger of an orchestral oboist's work becoming atrophied and stale. Chapter 1 emphasizes such considerations with a particular view on the sound of box-wood instruments – that is, the sound which eighteenth-century composers had in mind when composing for the oboe. If these differences are accepted in relation to the character-istic sound of the eighteenth-century orchestral woodwind section we have a good deal of adapting to do on modern in-struments. Yet this must be considered also in the light of the sound we must produce for a Mahler symphony or a Bartók orchestral piece.

One aspect of the solution rests in the use of a variable kind

143

of scrape for works of different periods and styles. This, however, is not as important as the concept itself, which informs the choice of an appropriate tone quality. The classical oboe had become a very refined instrument in the hands of Martini, the Bessozzis and Giuseppe Sammartini. Hawkins writes of the latter: 'He was a performer on the hautboy, an instrument invented by the French, and of small account, till by his exquisite performance, and a tone which he had the art of giving it, he brought it into reputation.' The qualities Mozart ascribed to Ramm are witness to the richness of sound these instruments produced. The more hollow, round tone was less differentiated from the flute, bassoon and clarinet than today. Until the '80s and '90s composers were not too unhappy about the interchanging of instrumental parts where specific players were not available in an orchestra. This must not be confused with the purely economic reasons for Mozart's prescribing a string quartet to accompany the soloist in some of his piano concertos, but simply that not all orchestras could boast the necessary instruments required in the woodwind, so that flute and oboe parts were often interchanged without complaint.

The orchestral role of the oboist in Haydn's early symphonies was often soloistic, the constitution of the wind section being two oboes, one bassoon and two horns. Oboists such as those of Prince Esterhazy's Court would have had no difficulty in blending with the smaller-sized horn of the 18th century in the mellow chords accompanying the strings in the *tutti* passages like those throughout Symphony No. 11 or Mozart's early G minor Symphony, No. 25. This horn produced a smaller and lighter sound than we hear in Strauss's orchestral works, which married beautifully with the delicate, round tone of the oboes. When clarinets, flutes and two bassoons enriched the woodwind section in the later years of Haydn's life, this marriage of unabrasive, sweet quality simply extended the blending which classical composers sought from the section. The interchangeability of clarinet/oboe and flute/oboe parts did not concern composers quite so much as would be the case today. The two versions of Mozart's G minor Symphony No. 40 attest to this; the first without, the second with clarinets.

In performing such works today it is this blending of sonorities which we must seek to achieve in the light, delicate colouring of the harmonic element.

There is a great difference in the quality of sound used in a chordal texture and a solo line. Vibrato needs to be limited to marry with the white sound of the horns. Any mannerism or heavy tone which obtrudes on to the strings in figurative sections detracts from the texture. Haydn's 'Harmony' Mass exemplifies this desire in that the woodwind and horns signify the title of the work by adopting the role of setting the harmonic textures throughout. Haydn, like most classical composers, saw the woodwind and horns in consort as the harmonic texture of a score in a rich backcloth for melodic elements in the strings. The quality of tone used for such works requires consideration with this in mind.

The two oboes are often featured as soloists in Haydn's early symphonies. No. 7, 'Le Midi', treats them as a *concertante* element, to the point where the second subject is devised specially for them. This work was composed with distinguished soloists such as the violinist Tomassini in mind, and Haydn never underestimated the qualities of his wind-players who always have elaborate, often demanding, parts to play. The second oboe is often equally as important as the first. In the slow movement of 'Le Coq' it is revealed as a solo line. For the principal player perhaps the best-loved example of Haydn's view of the oboe is in Symphony No. 96 (example 50).

Example 50

All the quotations describing the playing of Ramm and his contemporaries are of the utmost value in indulging the qualities of grace, lightness and beauty of sound, even to the point of a *tenuto* on the upbeat for the first repeat, continuing at a different dynamic. However, the beautiful *arpeggio* in the closing bars of the Trio needs lightness and clarity – and no trace of *rubato*. Haydn has been meticulous in requesting the first two notes as demi-semiquavers, not a vague quintuplet figure.

In the later symphonies of Haydn, the completely developed double woodwind section is fully-fledged. The twelve 'London' Symphonies of this period of production seem to surpass everything the composer had previously achieved, drawing the accolade from Rimsky-Korsakov that Haydn was the greatest orchestrator who ever lived – especially for wind. It is surprising, in view of this widely accepted view, that Haydn himself could say: 'I have only just learned in my old age how to use the wind instruments and now that I do understand them, I must leave the world.'

Apart from the London Symphonies, Haydn composed the Sinfonia Concertante Op. 84 in 1792, during his first visit to England. The use of the oboe is more or less conventional here and much in line with the common use of the instrument as a soloist in the orchestra. J. C. Bach, who had died in London a decade before, would have been gratified to hear the influences that worked on him in the slow movement of his Symphony in B♭, Op. 18 No. 2, echoing through Haydn's slow movement in this beautiful work.

Modern practical editions have moved a long way towards purifying the stylistic ingredients of Mozart and Haydn performances. Yet modern notation itself cannot truly indicate all the subtlety of nuance which the original manuscripts provide. This is especially true of Mozart. The Piano Concerto K. 491 is an outstanding example. Three kinds of staccato are indicated:

The first denotes a literal definition of *staccato*, i.e. 'detached', as distinct from 'very short'.

Example 51

Example 51 shows this in the context of several kinds of articulations and durations, the unqualified quavers and crochets requiring sustained sounds with minimum separation. The phrase reads as follows: a sustained anacrusis on the first note, those following with *staccato* dots to be played with a light articulation, but not too short; the final two quavers of the first bar are undotted, therefore, sustained. This creates a feeling for a second clause in the musical sentence. In other words, the *staccato* dots indicate a different characterization to the rest of the phrase, which is broader and more *cantabile* in mood.

Example 52

Example 52 is a kind of *staccato* used in *tutti* passages and rather bold. Mozart's vertical stroke demands as short a note as possible.

Example 53

Example 53 is an articulation derived from bowing, usually associated in Mozart with a motiv shared by violins and woodwind. Throughout this work it appears only on repeated note motivs: the manuscript uses a short-hand method in places: . It is a *cantabile* motiv which is more *quasi-legato* than *semi-legato*. The slightest separation is required, the expressiveness lying in the form of articulation. Taking care to avoid the exaggeration of a mannerism, the slightest *crescendo* may be made on each note after a very soft consonant attack:

Example 54

A variety of these forms can be found in sections such as example 54, where Mozart makes it very clear that many different forms of articulation are needed to achieve the expressiveness he requires.

This constant variation of articulation and nuance of phrasing is a hall-mark, not only of Mozart, but of all composers in the classical period. Although we cannot be expected to pursue the manuscripts of every piece we play, it is of paramount importance to consider each work in isolation from editorial marks, no matter how reliable the editor. The true style and individuality of a composer's expressive idiom will never be achieved at an artistic level of realization until such nuances become second nature in the performer's approach.

Seven

Playing Romantic Music

> 'Beethoven's music opens the floodgates of fear,
> of terror, of horror, of pain, and arouses that
> longing for the Eternal which is the essence of
> Romanticism. He is thus a pure Romantic composer'.
> E. T. A. Hoffmann, *Beethovens Instrumentalmusik*, 1813

I explained in Part I that Beethoven's life covered the transitional period between the classical two-keyed instrument and the early mechanized oboe. At the time of the first five symphonies and the opera 'Fidelio' two extra keys had been added to the two-keyed model. They would have helped the instrumentalist to negotiate some of the more tricky moments in these works, but the player of a four-keyed instrument would certainly have encountered one of the greatest challenges of his life when faced with the oboe solo in Florestan's aria in 'Fidelio' (example 55).

The hero is surrounded by his weeping family, and (as Berlioz explains it) 'mingles his tears of anguish with the broken sobs of the hautboy'. It is a highly emotional aria which requires something of a dramatic commitment from the oboist. After the slow introductory statement the rising arpeggios on falling intervals accompany the ecstasy of Fidelio's greetings for his family (a) full of animated cantabile. The 'sobs' appear at (b) when the union is complete, rising at (c) to yet more yearning arpeggios and the triumphant cascades up to top F at the end of the aria. There should be no fears for the modern oboist to dominate the tenor voice in this piece. It is a duet and requires all the projected richness of tone the player can produce. Restraint is required only at the beginning before the tenor enters. Here, it is not simply a question of a *piano espressivo*, but a need to conserve for the rise at the end of the first section. It is out of the question to take a breath until the first rest.

Example 55

Beethoven: 'Fidelio'

Beethoven chose the oboe for a very wide variety of musical characterizations:

Joy: The Scherzo of the Pastoral Symphony, where the syncopated theme so characteristic of the composer's middle period, courageously demands a repeat at a level of *pp* at the top of the instrument. Beethoven is sure-footed in orchestrating this with light strings in a lower register, so that the performer need have no fears of playing too quietly or too sweetly.

The Trio of the Scherzo in the Ninth Symphony, where the protracted legato solo is also subtly orchestrated to allow for a sustained *p* dynamic. Again, a delicate, sweet sound is called for, not a robust, virtuoso display. The carillon nature of the section calls for a sparkling briskness and delicacy which Beethoven seeks again and again from the oboe. Symphony No. 4 also abounds in such examples.

Nobility: Symphony No. 7 begins with the sonorous statement of the oboe solo, which calls for an entirely different sound and form of production. A free embouchure with maximum abdominal support and instrument held high creates the only possible conditions for projecting the glowing majesty of this statement.

Poignancy: The cadenza in the first movement of the Fifth Symphony bears great significance, not simply because it is a solo, but because it is the sole voice of melody, as opposed to rhythmic figuration, in this movement. The lone voice of the oboe halts the relentless repeated note rhythms to turn a simple phrase, and to change the course of the piece. Beethoven marks it *adagio* and *piano*, but not (as it would seem from many performances) *a piacere* or *ad lib*. As with all unaccompanied pieces, even in the 'fantasia' style of this phrase, the note values indicated by the composers should be observed unless instructed otherwise. Beethoven especially was meticulous about the nuance and exactitude of rhythmic inflexion. Unlike Couperin, he avoided prefaces, often choosing to supplement the notation of his works with profuse verbal explanations within the score. Therefore, we must think of the turn within the duration of the minim associated with it – slowly, but in time. My own preference is to sustain a sense of unity by making the crotchets approximately equal to the value of a whole bar of the Allegro. Too often this cadenza is made to sound like another piece wandering into the performance.

This same solemn voice of despair is chosen for the oboist as a 'concerto' performer in the slow movement of the Eroica Symphony. The repeated notes require separation (especially in a resonant hall) if the rhythm is to be discerned by the audience. *Tu tu-tu* is preferable to *tu tu-ru* for this end. The *acciacatura* needs to be carefully differentiated from the *appoggiatura* throughout, the former being very short but not accented, the latter taking full value of its written duration, and leaning (as C. P. E. Bach requires) with a slight emphasis at the expense of the long note following it. C. P. E. Bach is not too extreme a comparison here when it is considered that Beethoven sustained a very high regard for him, along with the influence he had on the younger composer's early work. The written *messa di voce* in the fourth complete bar of the solo attests to these early classical influences, which impinge on nineteenth-century music as late as the 1880s.

No doubt many more characteristics could be compiled to demonstrate Beethoven's use of the oboe in all its guises. That he set a mark on the instrument as an orchestral soloist in such a wide variety of expressive roles is an undoubted hallmark of the oboe's significance in the nineteenth-century orchestra. As a concerto performer enough minor works were written for the oboist by Spohr, Bellini and many lesser-known composers. However, as with all the woodwind family, it was the symphony orchestra which dictated the criteria for all aspects in the development of the mechanized instrument. It was the medium for which nineteenth-century composers considered the oboe best suited. In contrast there is a lamentable paucity of chamber music using the oboe.

After Beethoven, Berlioz was one of the main architects of this development. His 'Treatise' on the orchestra provides a valuable chart of possibilities (and impossibilities) of the mechanical instrument, reflecting the view above, that the oboe at this time did not suit the element of virtuoso display demanded of the concerto soloist. 'Rapid passages, chromatic or diatonic . . . produce an ungraceful and almost ridiculous effect . . . That which tempts solo-performers to use them in their fantasias or airs with variations goes but a little way to prove the contrary. The oboe is especially a melodic instrument: it has a pastoral character, full of tenderness – nay, I would even say, of timidity.' This is certainly the principal characteristic which comes through the works of Wagner, Brahms, Franck, Mendelssohn and Berlioz. In the 'Symphonie Fantastique' this characteristic is extended by the structural significance which Berlioz gives to dynamic range. Mozart and Haydn simply used *p* and *f*; Beethoven requires *pp* and *ff* with a wide range of accentuation; Berlioz, with an almost callous disregard for the double reed, asks for *ppp* followed immediately by a diminuendo in the second bar. Such demands may seem ordinary enough to the layman, but throughout this work the second oboist especially must demonstrate the highest qualities of control and facility in tone production. The G of the opening chord is required again at the close of the first movement with the same dynamic. Here, the problem is intensified by the exactitude required for placing the note not only *ppp* with the conductor's slow beat, but sensing as well the exact moment when the first oboist will fall to his new note from the previous bar. In such cases it is best to list the conditions of preparation:

1. Sub-divide the conductor's beat in your mind.
2. Breath on the minim upbeat with embouchure formed.
3. Enter as quietly as possible with the articulation, then swell very slightly once the sound appears. In this way you can gauge the attack simultaneously with the second violins.

Like the off-stage trumpeter in Beethoven's Overture 'Leonora' No. 3, who was accosted as a busker by the fire-warden during his solo in the outside corridors of the Royal Albert Hall, the off-stage oboe solo in the *Scène aux Champs* carries many similar anecdotes of wardens interrupting the Shepherd's Song with a stern, 'You can't do that there 'ere!' There is no indication from Berlioz that the oboist should be off-stage, but the convention is a worthwhile extravagance – especially in a cathedral where the space and long reverberation lend an added ethereal quality to the music; for nowhere else can be found a solo so apt to the composer's description of the oboe, which sings through every note of this exquisite movement.

The cor anglais too finds a haven of perfect characterization here. 'It has a melancholy, dreamy, and rather noble voice,' says Berlioz. He describes the shepherd's call, 'as the voice of a youth might reply to that of a young girl in a pastoral dialogue.' When this is repeated at the end of the movement without the answering call of the oboe, the composer explains that 'the dull accompaniment of the four kettledrums during the silence of the rest of the orchestra [creates] feelings of absence, of forgetfulness, of sorrowful loneliness, which arise in the bosoms of the audience on hearing this forsaken melody.' The feelings would 'lack half their power if played on any other instrument than the cor anglais.'

Example 56 (a) presents a tricky passage in the last movement which may be clarified in execution by conceiving it as in (b) (underlaid). The separation given by the inserted rests gives clarity to the articulations, especially with reiterated notes. The F♮ of the second triplet of bar 8 is worth noting.

In spite of his native lyricism, Berlioz was continually drawn by the strong currents of the Romantic movement in Germany. Like Schumann and Wagner, he was a writer as well as a composer. The significance of this lies in the fact that the Romantic movement was essentially a literary one, with strong foundations in an earnest philosophy which idealized Nature. Perhaps the literary quill that expressed this notion with the greatest clarity was that of Schopenhauer: 'In that it by-passes ideas, music is independent of the physical world – in fact, is completely ignorant of the physical world and could exist in a sense even if there were no world. This cannot be said of the other arts. Music is as direct an

Example 56 (a) and (b)

objectification and reflection of the entire Will as is the World itself . . .'

While space forbids me to elaborate on this, it is of the greatest importance to approach the towering genius of Wagner with an awareness of the supra-musical evaluations which motivated his art. His critics, among them Thomas Mann and Nietzsche, attest to the strength and danger inherent in the romantic spirit of Wagner's music, which demands a total abandonment to an ultra-aesthetic consciousness. He remains a figure of violent controversy – total worship, or total antipathy.

'Tristan and Isolde' is the apotheosis of this genre. Even after breaking with Wagner, Nietzsche could not free himself from the spell of this masterpiece: 'The world is a poor place for the man who has never been sick enough to enjoy this "ecstasy of Hell".' Within its pages the oboists and cor anglais players can discover some of the most rapturous music ever composed for the instruments, by a master who had precise ideas about the sounds he desired to hear, but at that time, few players who could muster those qualities. He requests that the same 'accomplished artist' who plays throughout the performance must also play the off-stage Shepherd's Tune at the beginning of Act 3.

Even more than Berlioz, Wagner depends greatly on a constant tide of dynamic variation in all his music. The ebb and flow; the sudden contrast diverting the passionate climax to yet new heights; the cascading fountains of flowing sound, are bigger than life in 'Tristan'. The Shepherd's Tune is a microcosm of the whole opera. Each bar is filled with dynamic nuance and figurative arabesque. The 'hairpin' dynamics should, if anything, be exaggerated to enhance the bitter loneliness of Tristan's wounded state, in contrast to the innocence of the shepherd playing his pipe.

These highspots of orchestral solos in the nineteenth-century repertoire do not concern the conductor-player relationship too much. The age of Berlioz, Wagner and Mendelssohn saw the rise of a new orchestral syndrome in the maestro-conductor who had absolute responsibility for the performance. The players experienced a variety of techniques from those mentioned above. Mendelssohn and Berlioz were incisive and precise in their beating, and both complained of Wagner's vagueness. Wagner's approach may well have resulted from his view that a composer's markings were never enough, and that the 'instinctive' interpretation of a 'musician of feeling' was the only sure route to the heart of any matter of interpretation. As a conductor he carried this to extremes in performances of Beethoven's Ninth Symphony by incorporating brass with the woodwind chords in loud passages. We cannot be accurate in judging such liberties because we are not able to assess with certainty why the woodwind sonority seemed unsatisfactory to him. The matter must be considered in the light of the intensive experimentation that went on during the development of mechanism between Beethoven's death and Wagner's active musical life. Wagner was convinced that Beethoven had to fight against the technical limitations of contemporary instruments. For someone who had only known the mechanized instruments in their early days this is an understandable reaction. It is, however, questionable whether such an idiosyncratic solution was wholly justified.

The magnitude of Wagner's subsequent influence on music is inestimable. The sweet-toned Lorée was fully evolved at the time of his death in 1883 – an instrument which the post-Wagnerites nourished with equally beautiful material. The oboe had come of age on a tide of glorious music which can never be surpassed in beauty and richness of expression.

Eight

20th Century Music: The Rise of the Solo Oboist

The neglect of the oboe as a concerto instrument in the nineteenth century is an unforgivable oversight of Fate! Was it due to the size of the vast symphony orchestra and the difficult odds this presented for the nineteenth-century instrument? Or was it due to the temporarily limiting factors of the mechanized oboe? No-one can tell. It is simply a badge of historical injustice that oboists must wear. This said, it must be stated that we have made up for it during my own lifetime with a vast solo and concerto repertoire comparable with most instruments. If it is the romantic element of which we are short, compensations do exist which, if not actually composed in Wagner's lifetime, do at least spring from the same well. One of the most important of these works is the Oboe Concerto of Richard Strauss. Composed as recently as 1947, the composer wrote the work in the twilight of his life, reliving the lush, perhaps rather over-ripe world of the 1890s – and none the worse for that!

The opening two minutes make more demands on breath control than any other work in the concerto repertoire. There is good reason for puzzlement that such an arch-orchestrator as Strauss could possibly compose a passage of continuous melody without a single natural break for breath. Whatever the reasons, we have to cope with the situation and take a stand over its solution. My own view is that oboe playing sounds unnatural and artificial if phrasing-through-breathing is absent from a performance. Therefore, I break the tied notes where necessary to breathe quickly through the nose. This can be made to sound perfectly natural if the phrasing of the semiquavers is approached with an inclination to make the first three notes of each figuration more deliberate. This helps to sustain continuity. Above all, the 'exercise' syndrome should be avoided. Before a breath is taken after a sustained tied note, the sound should be allowed to drop. Any abruptness must be avoided. After this opening the work presents no problems.

My brother Eugene's Concerto is, in many ways, more apposite for the oboe than the Strauss, belonging to the English pastoral school, reflected in similar works by Ralph Vaughan Williams, Cyril Scott and Rutland Boughton. Using a full orchestra as distinct from the chamber orchestra of the Strauss, the work contains some very delicate writing for percussion. In fact, the whole of the cadenza is accompanied by the sustained sound of a tam-tam with marvellous effect. The oboe is always audible above the rich textures. Today, the piece stands as a rewarding and effective work for the medium. Percy Grainger, another composer belonging to the group, once wrote to me in glowing terms after my premier performance of Cyril Scott's concerto: 'the greatest Oboe Concerto ever written . . .' No mean accolade from a fellow composer!

Unfortunately my first attempts to play the Vaughan Williams Concerto in 1944 were thwarted by the attacks of buzz-bombs, which closed down the Henry Wood Promenade Concerts for that year. It was finally premiered a year later with resounding success. This work, too, showed the oboe in all its guises from piping shepherd to brilliant virtuoso. Like the Strauss, it needs suppleness of rhythm and should never be rushed. The rehearsal for this performance presents a vivid picture in my mind of Vaughan Williams sitting on the platform as solid as a statue, holding an old-fashioned ear-trumpet, for all the world like a reincarnation of Beethoven.

Elgar, like Brahms, neglected to write a concerto for the oboe. However, in the 1920s I became a friend of the master – indeed, I taught him to drive a motor-car. Whether in gratitude for this, or for more serious musical reasons must remain one of those enigmas Elgar loved to create for his friends – but in 1931 he actually began to compose a Suite for Oboe. At this time he was ill with sciatica and only had a year or two more to live. So the sketches he made for the piece never advanced farther than the slow movement. The fly-leaf of the manuscript bore my name in Elgar's hand. His letter to me **(plate 15)** is evidence enough that he could barely put pen to paper at this stage. I chose my seventieth birthday, in 1967, to give the first performance of the single, magic movement.

Sir Donald Tovey, who transcribed a Bach Concerto for me to play on the oboe d'amore (see Discography, Appendix 4), also had some interesting things to say on the subject of the Double Concerto for Oboe and Violin. In a letter to me he wrote:

'By the way, I see that Peters have published an edition of the Concerto for Oboe and Violin, and that the editor has decided that it is in D minor. I am certain that he is wrong, not only because this would bring the oboe up to E, whereas Bach never writes above D, but because, if the original had not been in C minor, there would have been no conceivable reason why this

should become this

when the violin has to play it in a lower key.'

My performance of the Oboe d'Amore Concerto at the Usher Hall, Edinburgh provides another portrait for me, this time of Tovey. Waiting to go onto the platform, I was tied to my chair by this eccentric, but lovable scholar, while he strut-

PLATE THIRTEEN
Wrist motion required between a' (*top left*) and g' (*bottom left*)

PLATE FOURTEEN 18th century copy of Purcell Ode

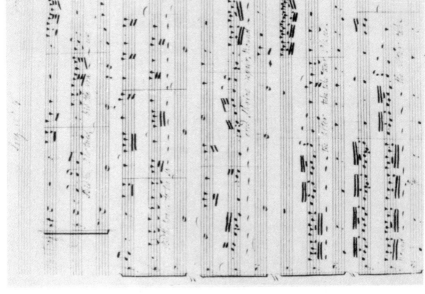

PLATE SIXTEEN Leon Goossens with Students in Finland, 1959.

ted up and down the green room like a priest at Mattins, talking incessantly about his ideas on the Bach manuscripts which led to his transcription. His evening dress, drab and old; his collar rat-bitten, and his hands deep in his pockets. He was a superb musician.

Recording

The supreme achievement of the oboe in the twentieth century lies in its reassertion as a soloist in the concerto medium. There is no doubt that the facilities of studio recording techniques have done much to encourage the effectiveness of this development. Any problems of balance are certainly diminished under recording conditions. Nevertheless, there are a few hazards inherent here which affect the oboe more than any other instrument, especially in relation to tone-quality. The control panel of the studio has enormous powers over the dynamics and relative balance of instruments when individual microphones are placed for each section or group of instruments throughout an orchestra or ensemble. Difficulties arise if the microphone is placed too close to the bell of the oboe. All the 'fundamental' sound of the rich, lower register will be enhanced at the expense of the clear, upper partials which play such an important part in the essentially clear, brilliant quality of characteristic oboe sound. The recorded tone under these conditions will be hollow and muted, and quite unlike the tone-quality of the individual player.

When I recorded the Vaughan Williams Concerto these conditions presented themselves to such a degree that I was in danger of knocking the microphone with my instrument. The complaint was made that my breathing was too audible and sounded like someone talking in the next room. What could I do about it? – came the query from the control room. My reply was short and to the point: 'You must move the microphone farther away!' Both problems were solved without further ado.

My very earliest experiences of recording were in the 1920s, when the bell of the oboe had to be directed into a large horn.

These recordings demonstrate a remarkable purity and clarity of tone in spite of the surface noise and occasional distortion. Joe Batten was the genius behind many of these Edison Bell recordings. His special effects were based on a highly sensitive musical response which produced some of the finest recordings ever made. In the 1930s a single microphone above the orchestra sufficed for recordings which include some that are now considered to be monumental. Today, our sophistication in the studio can be self-defeating if real collaboration is missing between the performing artist and the recording producer. Happily, the Vaughan Williams experience ended with a fine recording on all counts.

Other precautions for studio work must be maintained carefully. It is unforgivable for an instrumentalist to go into a recording studio with a clacking key. There is nothing a sound-controller can do about this; responsibility rests entirely with the performer.

Having stated that, I must now confess to one of the greatest clangers in the history of recorded sound!

We were in the studio to record Schumann's Cello Concerto with Piatigorsky as soloist. Like all artists he was capable of having an off-day, and on this occasion he was dissatisfied with his performance of the cadenza. I felt sympathy for him. After several attempts he finally decided to break and try later. When we had assembled again the recording producer recommended we do a rehearse run before making the recording. The tension was high and Piatigorsky played brilliantly, throwing off the cadenza with superb artistry. I was so carried away that I could not restrain myself from shouting 'Bravo' in a very loud voice. All was silence for a brief moment. Then the producer came into the studio, ashen-faced and full of despair. They had recorded it!

After the initial dismay had passed Piatigorsky said: 'I can't play it again'. But he had a simple solution: 'Simply put on the label

"CELLO – PIATIGORSKY

BRAVO! – GOOSSENS".'. . .

Orchestral Considerations

Intonation. The topic of intonation has been reserved for this chapter because I consider it to be of most importance in the context of orchestral playing. The problems are legion. An oboist must be constantly aware and assertive in arresting them as they arise.

(1) 'The strings are sharp!' The war-cry goes up and a familiar battle ensues. 'But we tuned to your A!' comes the response from the strings. It is usually a good-natured battle because the problems are manifest. The hall may be extremely hot, or scorching television production lights blazing down throughout rehearsal and concert. Invariably the pitch of the strings will rise. String players are naturally inclined to think on the bright side of a pitch because the sensation of the tone production seems vitalized by that edge of the note. Hot conditions intensify string tension so that the general pitch will gradually rise. The oboist will have pushed his staple in as far as possible. Without precautions for this contingency the player will have to bite and squeeze the reed to play as high a pitch as possible.

(2) Conversely, the orchestra may be performing in a stone cathedral in the arctic temperature of mid-winter. The single iron boiler glimmering with a feeble glow will be beyond the reach of your own comfort. Fingers freeze on the ice-cold metal of the keys, and the reed feels like a barb of ice on your lip. The only sustaining feature may be the beauty of the music being performed. The instrument will certainly play flatter than usual and the temporary warmth of breath will not induce it to rise.

A little help can be provided during rests: keep the instrument inside your jacket or cloak under warm armpits. A primitive ploy, but helpful!

(3) The orchestra could be touring a country where the pitch is higher than the frequency A = 440. If there is a piano concerto in the programme there is no salvation from the necessity to tune the orchestra to a high pitch for the whole programme; once settled, the pitch cannot be changed suc-

cessfully. We are creatures of habit! In spite of international agreements for the A 440 norm, some countries do persist with a higher pitch – a fact that must be accepted.

In the isolated instances relating to (1) and (2) it is important not to give way to general fluctuations of pitch too much. A strong wind section that will stick together over their own pitch can assert a firm anchor on intonation to the benefit of the orchestral texture. Ultimately, adaptation is a matter of discretion and sympathetic listening to other players. But the wind-players' assertion, while avoiding stubbornness, can be a strong influence on good general intonation. The oboist has a special problem here. The flute plays at the top of the texture. A sensitive player will have an ear for the bass of the ensemble (second bassoon or double-bass) to secure a good marriage of the outside pivots of the pitch and intonation. Generally, the oboist is active between these extremes and may have to act as a mediator in troubled times.

There are no rules for this aspect of the problem. The immediate qualification for a well-intoned wind section rests in tone quality. If there is a firm nucleus, or centre to the sound (a free-tipped reed supported by a firm heart), intonation problems are singled down to matters of aural sensitivity, along with the capacity of a player to maintain a flexible embouchure with reflexive response in correcting a discrepancy within a split second. Nobody can be right all the time.

Condition (3) has only one answer. An oboist should always have a few reeds in his store capable of playing at a sharp pitch. 70–71mm is a useful gauge. Experimentation with a shorter staple or a shorter cane length will tell individual players which is the best solution.

Reeds are a constant concern, but should never be confessed as a problem. I keep a supply well in hand and dismiss a reed after each concert. In this way a constant supply and reserve is created. Occasionally I will do a recital on a long-discarded reed that may not have been used for twenty years.

Fibre-glass reeds have been manufactured which can be useful in emergencies. However, they are by no means sensitive enough to replace the suppleness and dexterity of real cane.

Concluding remarks are often repetitive and disappointing. Therefore, I am using the expedient of quoting from a letter to me written by Sir Donald Tovey. He sums up all that is special to the oboe in a way that cannot be bette red :

'. . . the solo player . . . is ex-officio a singer. I am just getting up to the third act of "Parsifal" with some excellent local singers who are surprised to find that the meticulous Wagner, with all his wonderful orchestra markings, gives no marks whatsoever to the solo voices, except one "piano" (to prevent a single top note being misunderstood as a climax). How few modern composers there are who have the sense to *let you singers live on your breath*. Believe me.'   The italics are mine.

Nine

The Contemporary World
(by Edwin Roxburgh)

> '. . . the system of scales, modes, and harmonic
> tissues does not rest solely upon unalterable natural
> laws, but is at least partly also the result of aestheti-
> cal principles, which have already changed, and will
> still further change, with the progressive develop-
> ment of humanity.'
>
> Helmholtz

When cave-men discovered that sound could be produced by
blowing down a hollow bone, no amount of speculation could
conjecture that in tens of thousands of years' time this
phenomenon would still contain substance for further discoveries and novel disclosures. Yet that is the situation with
wind instruments today. Electronic means of propagating
sound have opened up to us the possibilities of applying the
whole audible frequency range to music-making, instead of
just the twelve semitones of the Western 'well-tempered'
tuning system. These developments have led players to take a
new look at their instruments. Originally designed to play
music for the diatonic idiom, physicists from Helmholtz's
time to the present day have taught us more and more that
this simple tube has a potential that begins to take on truly
staggering dimensions in sound capabilities well beyond those
already practised.

To identify the possibilities on all models would require a
book several times this size. Attempts to catalogue standard-
ized fingerings for all monophonic and multiphonic possibilities have been limited by the vast number and scope of the
variables from one mechanical system to another. The organi-
zation of vents and speaker mechanisms from model to
model creates opposing forms of overtone realizations. The
Italian composer Bruno Bartolozzi did pioneer work in
researching the field. With his colleagues, he has documented

fingering possibilities which apply to a specific mechanical system. Difficulties arise when these fingerings are attempted on alternative models. Standardization is impossible, and the beginner must recognize that solutions may not be found readily from specific charts. The following essay attempts to deal with the wider application of the new techniques as they present themselves in individual works. The purpose here is to introduce study methods for the interpretation of the new and growing repertoire displaying them.

Embouchure and Reed

It has already been stated that the embouchure provides a mobile support for the reed in all performing circumstances. For the extended technical demands of most contemporary music, this precept is even more imperative. Breath-support, articulation and embouchure in relation to an easy-speaking reed require a sensitivity more refined than ever before for response to the subtle harmonics of multiphonic production, high register pianissimo, flutter-tonguing and *glissando* passages. The reeds required for the solo repertoire in this genre are best considered with these objectives in mind. Above all, they must not be too heavy. Too much wood and too long a scrape will not provide sympathetic conditions for the high register notes or for effective flutter-tonguing. Less wood in the reed than usual will certainly produce a slightly thinner sound, which many players might consider too much to ask. There is no compromise. Players approaching this part of the repertoire for the first time are well-advised to begin with a very easy reed. Facility and ease of production diminish the problems by half, and the conditions of the embouchure for less conventional demands will gradually mature to compensate for any thinness initially experienced. The embouchure is best considered in the context of each piece.

Perhaps the most drastic of manoeuvres relates to extreme high notes. Example 57 aims a minor third above the accepted upper register of the oboe. At *a'''* we tend to call it a day. The instrument is, however, capable of pro-

Example 57

Roxburgh *Ecclissi*

ducing a chromatic scale with true expressive tone up to
c''''. Both fingers and embouchure must take unconventional
steps. The chromatic fingering from *a'''* is shown in **fig. 18.**

Figure 18

(3) ♩	(3) ♩	(3) ♩	(3) ♩
●	●—(○)	○	○
○	○	●	●
●	● G♯	● B♮	○
○	○	●	●
●	●	●	●
○	E♭ ○	C ○	C ○

The *a'''* may be produced with a normal embouchure; *b'''*
requires an adjustment.

Consider that the reed, as generator of the sound, maintains a vibratory system independent of, as well as adjacent
to, the oboe. Like any vibratory medium it is activated by a
mode of attack – in this case, air and embouchure. Played
without the instrument the reed will make a croak at the pitch
b'. If any part of the medium (the cane) is prevented from
responding by being stifled, the wave forms being propagated
will be shorter, and the resultant sound higher. A simple
experiment may clarify the issue: place the reed alone between
the lips without forming an embouchure. Very gently, and
without pressure, place the upper and lower teeth evenly at
the base of the scrape. Close the embouchure without
folding the lips and blow gently, providing enough resistance

with the teeth to prevent the air from pushing the reed away. A sound almost one octave higher than the normal croak will be produced because only that part of the reed behind the teeth (the scrape) is being activated. When used for the extreme high register this embouchure will produce the notes with clarity, ease and good intonation.

For isolated notes in this register alternative fingerings are available which provide a firmer quality:

Figure 19

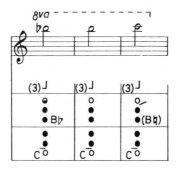

$b\natural''''$ and c'''' require the forefinger, left hand, to be placed on the second finger-hole to allow the second finger to activate the $c\sharp$ trill key.

Sustaining a Sound while Breathing-in

On pp. 5–6 Berlioz is quoted in a rather ungenerous description of an Indian Ottu-player who could breath in through his nose while sustaining the sound of his instrument. This feature has not been a common facet of oboe technique until recent times. Nevertheless, it has occasionally been called for in passages such as the off-stage Cor Anglais solo in Wagner's 'Tristan and Isolde'. Bate describes the conductor, Richter's admiration and surprise when Charles Reynolds performed this solo with no apparent break for breath. We may assume that Reynolds had perfected this form of nose-breathing.

A reed with an easy response is required in order to

produce an appropriately light embouchure. Collect as much air in the cheeks as possible by placing the tongue in an arched position as if for a gutteral 'g'. In this way the back of the tongue can act as a gate of pressure for the locked air, while the lip pushes slowly upwards towards the roof of the mouth, directing the air with strong pressure into the reed. In this way the air in the cheeks is unable to escape into the throat cavity, being isolated from the breathing channel between the nose and wind-pipe. While the tongue is pushing air the normal breathing process through the nose can be activated.

This is easier said than done. Exercises should be performed without the reed at first; then with the reed alone, and finally with the reed in the instrument. With an easy reed the knack can be accomplished fairly quickly. Using a 'teeth' embouchure (see p. 168) can be helpful on extreme high notes.

Single Sounds

(1) *Harmonics* The conventional range of notes on the oboe is derived from a system of fundamental pitches in the lower register, and harmonics (overtones) derived from these for the upper range. These are natural harmonics extending above a fundamental on the series: octave, 12th, 15th, 17th and 19th. All basic fingerings have been derived from these constants, but they do not constitute the only combinations possible. It is these variables that composers have been stimulated to explore in recent years, for they expose latent possibilities in wind instruments which have been accepted in string-playing for centuries. By stopping a string to create an alternative fundamental the string-player can produce an artificial harmonic by touching a nodal point elsewhere with another finger. In a similar way, the oboist can create an artificial harmonic by using an alternative fingering for a fundamental sound. However, this fundamental will establish a different harmonic series because it is not based on the natural fundamentals of the instrument. Even this over-simple explanation will indicate that the monophonic possibilities of the instru-

ment become increased by the hundred. The immediate characteristic of these variable fundamental fingerings is apparent in highly contrasted tone-colours and dynamics, created by the suppression of the natural harmonics of the tone in favour of the upper partials of unnatural derivation.

The note *b'* permits the greatest number of fundamental fingerings which, because of the various series of partials for each, provide not only a wide contrast of colour, but dynamic contrasts as well. **Figure 20** shows some of these fingerings which are universal to all instruments:

Figure 20

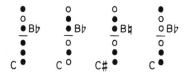

Berio's 'Sequenza VII' exploits this remarkable phenomenon in an exhaustive essay exploring its possibilities. The potentials of the note are emphasized by the sustained presence of the *b'* on an oscillator throughout the piece. A pistol crack *fff* at the beginning is reduced to *ppp* within four seconds – an indication of the constantly wide dynamic range to be expected. Each *b'* is qualified by a number in a circle, indicating a particular fingering for each articulation in accordance with a key provided by Heinz Holliger, the work's dedicatee. There are five fingerings, apart from the open, standard version. They represent various fundamental versions for each number. Holliger's recommendations work well if the instrument is similar in system to a Gillet Conservatoire model. However, any system which keeps the left hand first-finger plate closed permanently will not be suitable for playing this music, except by compromising with the use of the limiting combinations of right hand fingers which can colour the standard open note.

Different models may require slight modifications of the fingerings provided, but the following group is constant **(fig. 21):**

Figure 21

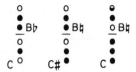

The fingerings indicated by the numbers imply a variety of timbres as well as dynamics. They are especially effective on a sustained sound containing several changes of fingering. Any modifications made for individual models must take this into account.

Example 58

Example 58 indicates the recommended fingering:

for 4, which, on some models, will produce d'''. This will not do, of course. A dark, soft sound is required.

A modified fingering is perfectly acceptable if it produces the desired effect.

The vocal characteristics of the oboe are especially evident in contemporary music. These aspects of colouration and sudden changes of timbre are much akin to the kaleidoscopic effect of multiple-vowel formations in Stockhausen's 'Stimmung' for voices. This comparison with Berio's 'Sequenza VII' stretches into the exploration of the harmonic series with a similar artistic intention.

Although provisions for individual models are not explored, Bartolozzi provides and discusses fingering charts for other single notes.

(2) ***Vibrato, Quarter-tones and Note-bending*** *Vibrato* has been explained in Chapter 4. The topic arises again here because we have not yet coined a word for describing the kind of expression which requires a positive change of frequency on a single sustained note. *Vibrato* is as good a word as any other, as long as we maintain the distinctions associated with its application in various kinds of music. In the contemporary field a form of exaggerated vibrato is often associated with inner rhythmic motivs and may be very slow, very fast or progressively slower or faster. When associated with 'hairpin' dynamics the effect is often magical (example 59).

Example 59

Holliger *Siebengesang*

A simple lip oscillation moving the jaw up and down, is required for all of these forms.

Using the same kind of lip movement, 'note-bending' can be achieved. This is a form most frequently used in jazz. It is too familiar to require further explanation.

A more positive form of note alteration is found in a work by Klaus Huber (example 60):

Example 60

Huber *Noctes Intelligibilis Lucis*

The exquisite poignancy of this phrase set against the shuddering harpsichord tones can only be achieved if each note is a well-intoned quarter-tone. With the use of the wing keys and smaller vent keys in association with standard fingerings, each chromatic interval on the oboe can be altered by a quarter-tone below or above. The symbols commonly used for this purpose are:

        ‡ 1/4 – tone sharp
        # 3/4 – tone sharp
        ♭ 1/4 – tone flat
        ♭ 3/4 – tone flat

The fingering for example 60 is shown in **fig. 22**:

Figure 22

Fingering charts are available for quarter-tone fingerings, but they present a very idiosyncratic approach. The subject defies any dogmatic attempt at standardization. The approach recommended above along with experimentation with wing-keys **(fig. 22)** will save many frustrations when the charts fail to induce an instrument to make the desired sounds.

Quarter-tone fingering is useful in negotiating a finger-*vibrato*. This is associated with the '*flattement*' ornament of the eighteenth century (see page 109). For example 61 use forked F fingering for the first note, and trill on the appropriate notes with the E♭ key.

Example 61

(3) *Glissandi* Among works using *glissandi* are Klaus Huber's 'Noctes', discussed above, and Richard Rodney Bennett's Oboe Concerto.

Example 62 (a) and (b)

Example 62 needs ascending and descending forms. The combined agency of embouchure and fingers are required to accomplish a smooth progression. The fingers take their cue from the clarinettist's practice of drawing the fingers slowly off the keys at a sideways angle. The embouchure assists at points where the fingers are unable to manipulate smoothly across a break. With open ring mechanism the problem does not extend beyond the clarinettist's procedure. With the covered rings of the modern Gillet system oboe, difficulties arise. A Conservatoire model should approach example 62 (a) with the following manoeuvres: play bb'' with key Sp covered with the left hand forefinger; slide the second finger left hand upwards exposing the vent slowly, then raise the key; the same motion is required for key Sp before the left hand forefinger is released, with a slight relaxation of the lips to arrive at $c\#'''$ with the following fingering:

Figure 23

```
    L
    o
    o
    o
   ───
    ●
    o
    o
```

Gradually tighten the embouchure while releasing the right hand forefinger to finger d''' authentically. The assistance of the embouchure over the firmer harmonics is essential over the whole range.

The descending version is more difficult to play – a fact recognized by the composer in example 62 (b) where only a tone is required. Begin by withdrawing the reed to flatten the pitch by embouchure; then approach the second ring (left hand) from above and place the key down slowly before covering the central vent. Alternatively, play *b″* as follows:

Figure 24

```
        L
        o
        ●
        o
       ───
        o
        o
        o
```

closing the finger-plate initially with the first finger before drawing it over the vent. Both methods require embouchure assistance.

The effect of an oboe *glissando* should never be crude, unless the style of the piece demands it. The compositional impulse behind such a gesture is akin to the eighteenth-century '*accent*' (see page 109), and implies an expressive inflection.

(4) ***Flutter-tonguing*** This has been a standard procedure since Stravinsky indicated it in 'The Rite of Spring'. There are two approaches. (a) Incline the reed towards the upper lip; roll the tongue behind the upper teeth so that a trill is created by the area underneath the tip, rolling lightly against the reed, while allowing air to be emitted between the lower blade of the reed and the lower lip. Play towards the tip of the reed. (b) Using a closed embouchure perform a guttural 'r' with the back of the tongue against the soft palate.

(5) ***Rolling Tone*** Klaus Huber introduces an interesting sound, shown in example 63. This is produced by gripping the reed

Example 63   Huber *Noctes..*

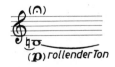

(*D*) *rollender Ton*

Klaus Huber: 'Noctes . . .'

firmly at the base, allowing the tips of the blades to over-react to the vibrations so wildly that the tone becomes inter-mittent in a rolling sound.

Multiphonic Procedures

Throughout an oboist's years of training much of the time is spent in purifying tone-quality and resisting those extra resonances that so often creep into a sustained tone. The fact that the instrument is highly susceptible to the vibration of several frequencies at a time within the single air column is a problem to be overcome in the diatonic/melodic music of the past. However, in the age of electronic resources and the vast new field that sound exploration has discovered, the great potential of alternative sound productions in wind instruments has become a topic of increasing interest to composers and performers. Now that musicians are exploring sound spectra with intense concern for colour and nebulous fields of pitch, the oboe has a beautiful and important con-tribution in this creative arena. Multiple frequencies are now a source of instrumental cultivation which bring composers flocking to those instrumentalists who seek to perfect the techniques associated with their development.

Multiphonic articulations (or chords) require much more suppleness of embouchure than single sounds. The following examples will serve as a basis for explanation of some of these possibilities.

Chords derived from relaxation of lip pressure on a single note (fingering illustrations are adjacent to each example):

Example 64

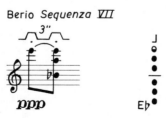

Berio *Sequenza* VII

Normal lip pressure should be used. With the relaxation of the lower lip the chord will appear.

Example 65

Roxburgh *Ecclissi*

When the chord is based on the sounding fundamental the lip pressure must be very relaxed to begin with. The single note will appear when a firm grip is asserted.

Homogeneous Chords

Example 66

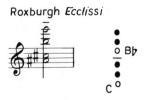

Roxburgh *Ecclissi*

Example 66 indicates two important elements in the finger positions which produce a host of chords.

The left hand keeps the B♭ key down, increasing the effective length of the vibrating column by closing the lower holes of the pipe. This in itself produces a wide range of quietly-produced upper partials. By keeping open the left hand third finger-hole, the long vibrating column is interrupted by the sympathy this vent will attract from other harmonics. The right hand position uses a combination which is the basis for many possibilities as well, the closing of the C key assisting in the closing of the whole length of the pipe at the bell, venting the third finger-hole. With all models, combinations of fingerings based on these principles will produce innumerable chords in a galaxy of colours from *ppp* to *fff*, harsh and sweet. A firm grip at the base of the reed is required.

Homogeneous Chords Mixed with Single Notes

Example 67

Roxburgh *Ecclissi*

This is perhaps the simplest of all chord productions to achieve. The reed is already vibrating responsively from the single note, so that the chord appears without change of embouchure at the sudden displacement of the chord fingering.

Double Harmonics

Amongst the most widely-used multiphonic possibilities are double harmonics in fifths. There is a hushed, ethereal quality in these sounds. Perhaps the ghosts of Delphic hymns and medieval organum haunt our imaginations in the presence of perfect fifths – an interval that pervades the structure of all modes of musical language. Whatever the case, the effect of this interval is unique when produced as double harmonics on the oboe.

Example 68

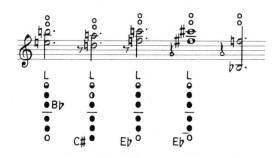

Niccolo Castiglioni: 'Alef'

Example 68 is taken from an unaccompanied piece which allows plenty of time for each articulation to speak easily.

179

Difficulties in achieving security for these sounds rest in the fact that lip – and air – pressure must be gauged to attract two harmonics from a fundamental which must itself be cancelled from the sound. The nodal points in the vibrating column have to be subtly sensitized. For this reason production is easier without a tongued attack, relying on breath-pressure to produce the sounds and on lip-pressure to secure them. Tight lips across the teeth (especially the lower) and a firm grip at the base of the scrape will set the conditions for production.

The fifth chord contains the fundamental and is easier to produce. Use standard fingering for *b*♭, press the reed hard against the lower lip using the same kind of embouchure as above, and incline the sound towards the upper note, allowing the fundamental to 'breathe' through. This can only be produced successfully at a low dynamic.

Example 69

Berio *Sequenza VII*

Where double harmonics are tied to an anacrusis the problem of attack is not quite so acute, because the air column is already functioning before the lip adjustment has to be made.

Example 70

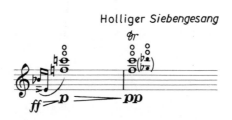

Holliger *Siebengesang*

Berio *Sequenza VII*

Example 70 shows an effective trill. Reference to the fingerings in example 68 will show that a trill with the F key is all that is necessary here. Example 71 requires an extension of the ploy by producing the trill a semitone higher. Sustain the fingering for the fourth chord of example 68 and trill with the middle finger right hand.

Electronics and General Considerations

Considerations of variable timbres, including the prism of sound created by difference tones from the crossing paths of high harmonics, are areas for wide examination. This brief introduction to the field can only touch on a technical approach.

The acoustic properties of the oboe take on new proportions of creative potential when amplification and other electronic resources are added. Heinz Holliger has led the field here with works such as 'Cardiophonie', in which a contact-microphone is placed against the performer's chest to amplify the heart-beat and sound of breath. This is fed through a ring-modulator which reproduces the sound while the player pursues the oboe part. In his 'Siebengesang' the oboe is fitted with a crystal microphone connected to a circuit which reaches a loudspeaker through a transformer, sound mixer, reverberation chamber and amplifier. With this added dimension such effects as key-tapping and blowing a bare staple without cane in the instrument, take on a truly musical purpose. The sound of overblowing to the fourth harmonic of B♭ cannot be heard without the aid of the sound mixer.

In all periods of music history fashion tends to breed

181

gimmickry. But in 'Siebengesang' we find what some may call simply 'tricks' put to the very highest artistic purpose.

All this seems a long way from the tuneful art pursued by oboists in the past. The music composed for the instrument since Beethoven has concentrated mainly on its lyrical qualities with good reason. This quality can never be abandoned because it is the true nature of oboe sound. It is the language of music itself that constantly changes, and instruments have always been adapted to these transformations. That we have a host of new sound sources and means of propagating sound with electronics is an exciting and challenging prospect for both composer and instrumentalist alike. The graphic means of conveying a stylistic concept are equally difficult today as they were in the eighteenth century. For the modern oboist a departure from tradition was first established in Stockhausen's Wind Quintet, 'Zeitmasse', composed in 1956. To match the number of players the work is based on a series of five different time-measures, sometimes sounding all at once, at other times in succession. The twelve tempi are interlaced with accelerandi and rallentandi to specific metres within the tempo gauge. The players must learn these tempi. Once digested, the free, or aleatoric, passages, where players do not have to co-ordinate their articulations, can be played with the utmost virtuosity and brilliance. The facility and vitality demanded of this music, along with its wide-ranging 'melodic' passages is characteristic of many composers of this period, all of whom require this sense of virtuosity and panache. While the notation in 'Zeitmasse' is exact in its rhythmic and durations intentions, the aleatoric elements have subsequently become free in notation, leaving far more to the judgement and taste of the performer. (The echoes of eighteenth-century extemporization are not inappropriate.)

These expressive inclinations have not been the substance of any one school of composition. In a more traditional guise Benjamin Britten presents the characteristics of rhythmic contraction and rarefaction found in 'Zeitmasse' in his 'Six Metamorphoses after Ovid', composed in 1951. The first of these, 'Pan', calls for a true sense of improvisation from the player, in imitation of the pan-pipes on which the figurations are designed (examples 72 and 73)

Example 72

Example 73

Britten: Six Metamorphoses after Ovid

In a similar way Klaus Huber has composed the *rallentando* shown in example 73 with closing ligatures thus (example 74):

Example 74

Perhaps a more improvisatory way of showing a similar intention.

With the Britten work, it is extremely important not to confuse the improvisatory gestures with the style of more recent works by composers using spatial notation. The above example is an isolated instance, for Britten is explicit in his tempi and notational instructions. All matters of interpretation must respect them.

The ultimate path of the 'serial' technique Stockhausen used in 'Zeitmasse' led to a more open-ended form of notation which is described above as spatial. Rather than notating the uncertain displacement of notes between one point and another, composers have tended to adopt a form which gives greater scope of freedom to the individual performer's capacity for virtuosity and imaginative interpretation. The apogee of this style is in Berio's 'Sequenza VII'. Comparisons with examples 73 and 74 can be made. The notes in Example 75 are displaced approximately in relation to their spatial disposition within the measure.

Example 75

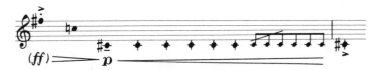

Berio: 'Sequenza VII'

These stylistic elements are amply demonstrated in orchestral works such as the same composer's 'Epiphonie', where improvisatory material is established in boxes. However, to explore this repertoire, along with the many other areas of consideration, would require another book.

In examining some of the major propensities of the oboe in this volume it may be seen that our sights are broadening into the past as well as the future. The composer's preoccupations in relating the abstract substance of musical sound to graphic symbols provides a challenging quest for the performer, whether in eighteenth-century or twentieth-century music.

A discriminating approach towards new music is the most important contribution an oboist can provide. This reflects a statement at the beginning of the book which explains the essential nature of collaboration between composer and performer: 'It is not always the composer who has necessarily extended the expressive and technical range of the instrument at his own whim, so much as the individual players, who have demonstrated uncatalogued skills to the composer.'

Here lies the future.

Appendix I

A list of manufacturers

England: Boosey and Hawkes Ltd, London; T. W. Howarth, London; Rudall Carte, London.

France: Buffet, Paris; Leblanc (Noblet), Paris; Lorée (Cabart), Paris; Rigoutat, Paris.

West Germany: Adler; Kreule, Tubingen; Puchner.

East Germany: Markard; Monnig; Ubel.

Italy: Ignagnoli, Rome; Orsi, Milan; Prestini, Milan; Santoni, Como.

U.S.A.:   Fox, New York; Conn, Elkhart; Laubin, New York; Lesher, Elkhart; Linton, Elkhart.

Appendix II

The Oboe Repertoire

The oboe repertoire in published form is a strange mixture of brilliant masterpieces together with inane rubbish. Therefore, in the following list, arrangements and unworthy editions of eighteenth-century works have been omitted in an attempt to represent a wide range of original music for the oboe at its best.

In a selective list of this kind some important works are bound to be left out. No claim is made for an exhaustive research. Among the finer works consciously omitted are many that rest in museums in first editions only (e.g. two Sonatinas by T. A. Walmisley in the British Museum) and many contemporary works awaiting a publisher.

The comments are designed to assist programme planning and not as expressions of personal taste.

Abbreviations

Al. Fl.	Alto Flute	Fl.	Flute
Bc.	Bass Continuo	Guit.	Guitar
Bsn.	Bassoon	Hcd.	Harpsichord
C.A.	Cor Anglais	Hn.	Horn (French)
Cb.	Double Bass	Hp.	Harp
Cl.	Clarinet	O.	Orchestra
ed.	Edited by	Ob.	Oboe

The authors and publishers have endeavoured to ensure that the information in this section is complete but some omissions are unavoidable.

Ob. d'am.	Oboe d'Amore	Tne.	Trombone
Org.	Organ	Tni.	Timpani
Pic.	Piccolo	Tpt.	Trumpet
Pno.	Piano	Va.	Viola
S.O.	String Orchestra	Vc.	'Cello
Tamb.	Tambourine	Vn.	Violin

Solo Oboe (including works with magnetic tape)
All works in this category are twentieth-century compositions, with a bias towards virtuosic display.

Arbatsky, Y. Sonata. Zimmermann.

Arma, P. Soliloque. Billaudot.

Arnold, M. Fantasy. Faber.

Apostel, H. E. Sonatine Op. 39a. U.E.

Antinion, T. 5 Likes (Ob. d'am.). Bärenreiter.

Bartolozzi, B. Collage. Zerboni.

Berio, L. Sequenza VII. U.E.

Birtwistle, H. Chanson de Geste (+ tape). U.E.

Bozza, E. Suite Monodique. Leduc.

Britten, B. Six Metamorphoses After Ovid. Boosey & Hawkes.

Castiglioni, N. Alef. Ars Viva Verlag-Mainz.

Dobrowolski, A. Music For Magnetic Tape And Oboe (simplified score for soloist with record of tape part). P.W.M.

Exton, J. Three Pieces. Chester.

Fillipi, A. de. Ex Tempore. Gen. Music. Pub. Co.

Gaslini, G. Seguali Für Oboe. U.E.

Globokar. A Tenstudie for oboe with throat and contact microphone.

Holliger, H. Cardiophonie (+ tape). Schott.

Kotonski, W. Monochromia. P.W.M.

Krenek, E. Sonatina. Bärenreiter.

LeFanu, N. Soliloquy. Novello.

Maderna, B. Solo per oboe, musetta, corno inglese, oboe d'amore (solo esecutore). Ricordi.

Mihalovici, M. Melopeia Op. 102. Billaudot.

Müller, G. Sonata. Sikorski.

Patterson, P. Monologue. Weinberger.

Rainier, P. Pastoral Triptych. Schott.

Renosto, P. Ar-Loth, per oboe, corno ingleo, oboe d'amore. Ricordi.

Schenker, F. Monolog. Veb deutscher verlag für musik Leipzig.

Sigtenhorst-Meyer, B. Landelijke Miniaturen (3 Suites). Alsbach.

Sigtenhorst-Meyer, B. Sonatine. Alsbach.

Singer, L. Work for Solo Oboe. Zerboni.

Stockhausen, K. Solo (+ Rückopplung). U.E.

Stockhausen, K. Spiral (Oboe mit Kurzwellenempfanger). U.E.

Szalonek, W. Quattro Monologhi. P.W.M.

Weber, A. Synecdoque. Leduc.

Wellesz, E. Suite. Bronde.

Oboe and Piano

The aim here is to provide a selection of recital pieces composed originally for oboe and piano (plus an odd few for organ).

A variety of periods and styles is covered including:

A substantial concert pieces in traditional idioms

B short characteristic works suitable as preludes to a concert

C interesting period pieces (e.g. Triébert – a name more closely associated with making *oboes* (rather than pieces) in the nineteenth century

D modern works acknowledged as avant garde

B. Addison, J. Inventions/Rhapsody/Prologue. O.U.P.

A Arnold, M. Sonatina. Lengnick.

B Arrieu, C. Impromptu. Leduc.

B Auric, G. Impromptu. Noël-Gallet.

B Badings, H. Canzona (organ). Donemus.

A Bennett, R. R. Sonata. Mills.

A Berkeley, L. Sonatina. Chester.

B Bessozzi, A. Sonata in C. Chester.

B Bessozzi, A. Sonata in D. Schott.

A Boismortier, J. de. Sonata in E min. Bärenreiter.

A Boutry, R. Sonatine. Salabert.

A Bowen, Y. Sonata Op. 85. Chester.

B Bozza, E. Lied (C.A.). Leduc.

A Breville, P. de. Sonatine. Ronart.

B Breville, P. de. Maneh (C.A.). Leduc.

B Bush, A. Northumbrian Impressions. Novello.

A Dalby, M. Sonatina. Novello.

C Donizetti, G. Sonate. Peters.

A Dubois, P. M. Sonatine (C.A.). Leduc.

B Dukas, P. Alla Gitana. Leduc.

A Dutilleux, H. Sonate. Leduc.

A Evans, P. Sonata. Chester.

B Fauré, G. Piece. Leduc.

B Franck, C. Piece V. Leduc.

B Goossens, E. Islamite Dance (3). Leduc.

B Grovlez, G. Saraband and Allegro. Leduc.

A Hindemith, P. Sonata. Schott.

B Horder, M. Sussex Folk Tune with 6 Variations (ed. L.G.). Peters.

A Hovhaness. Sonata for 2 Oboes and Organ Op. 130. Peters.

A Horovitz, J. Sonatina Op. 3. Mills.

D Iliff, J. Syzygy. Int. Mus. Co. Ltd.

A Jacob, G. Sonatina (Pno. or Hcd.). Rumanian State Publishing House.

D Krenek, E. Four Pieces. Bärenreiter.

D Krenek, E. Sonatina. Rougwen Music.

C Lalliet, T. Fantaisie Originale (C.A.). Costallat.

C Lalliet, T. First Concert Solo. Costallat.

C Leschetitzky, T. Variations on a Theme of Beethoven. Schott.

B Malipiero, G. F. Impromptu Pastoral. Leduc.

A Malipiero, G. F. Sonata. Zerboni.

A Milhaud, D. Sonatine. Durand.

B Neilson, C. Zwei Fantasiestücke. Hansen.

B Pierné, G. Serenade. Leduc.

A Piston, W. Sonata. Augener.

A Poulenc, F. Sonata. Chester.

D Ranki, G. Don Quijote y Dulcinea. E.M.B.

B Reger, M. Romance in G. Breitkopf & Härtel.

B Reizenstein, F. 3 Concert Pieces Op. 11. Boosey & Hawkes.

A Reizenstein, F. Sonatina. Lengnick.

B Richardson, A. French Suite. O.U.P.

B Rivier, J. Improvisation and Final. Leduc.

A Rubbra, E. Sonata in C Op. 100. Lengnick.

B Roussel, A. Aria. Leduc.

E Roxburgh, E. Images. U.M.P.

E Roxburgh, Aulodie for oboe, oboe d'amore and piano. U.M.P.

A Saint-Saens, C. Sonata. Durand.

B Sammartini, G. Sonata in G. Chester.

A Schollum, R. Sonatine. Augener.

D Schuller, G. Sonata. McGinnis.

D Searle, H. Gondoliera (C.A.). Schott.

D Seiber, M. Improvisation. Schott.

C Spohr, L. Andante and Variations Op. 34. Peters.

A Stanley-Smith, D. Sonata. S.P.A.M.

C Triébert, C. Air Varié. Lemoine.

D Tiệt, Ton-That. Cinq Pièces. Transatlantique.

A Vanhall, J. Sonata. McGinnis.

B Wilkinson, P. Suite. Novello.

A Wordsworth, W. Theme and Variations Op. 57. Lengnick.

Oboe and Harpsichord – 20th Century

These pieces are useful as twentieth-century items in a baroque ensemble programme. The work by Huber is discussed in Chapter 9.

Dodgson, S. Suite in D. O.U.P.
Huber, K. Noctes Intelligibilis Lucis. Schott.
Maconchy, E. Three Bagatelles. O.U.P.
Tiêt, Ton-That. Hy Vong 267 (C.A.). Transatlantique.

18th Century for Oboe(s) with Bass Continuo
(Oboe and Bass-continuo unless otherwise stated)

Where practical editions are not available in urtext form, alternative publication, produced by reputable editors have been selected.

C.M. = Collegium Musicum
H.M. = Hortus Musicus
N.M.A. = Nagels Musik-Archiv

Albinoni, T. Sonata in A minor. Bärenreiter.
Babell, W. Sonatas in F minor and G minor. O.U.P.
Babell, W. Sonata in B♭. Sikorski.
Bach, C. P. E. Sonata in G minor (C.M.). Breitkopf & Härtel.
Bach, J. C. Quintet in D (Fl. Ob. Vn. Vc. Bc.) (H.M.). Bärenreiter.
Bach, J. C. 6 Quintets Op. 11 (Fl. Ob. Vn. Va. Bc.) No. 1 in C; No. 2 in G; No. 3 in F; No. 4 in E♭; No. 5 in A; No. 6 in D. Bärenreiter.
Danican-Philidor, A. Sonata in D minor (H.M.). Bärenreiter.
Forster, C. Sonata in C minor. Eulenberg.
Galuppi, B. Trio Sonata in G (Ob. Vn. Bc.). Bärenreiter.
Galuppi, B. Trio Sonata in G (Fl. Ob. Bc.). Bärenreiter.
Geminiani, F. Sonata in E minor (H.M.). Bärenreiter.
Graun, C. H. Trio Sonata in F (Ob. Vn. Bc.). Breitkopf & Härtel.
Handel, G. F. Urtext edition of all solo sonatas and sonatas for 2 Obs. in preparation (H.M.). Bärenreiter. Otherwise Chrysander's Gesselschaft, or Peters.
Heinichen, J. D. Sonata for 2 Oboes and Bc. Breitkopf & Härtel.

Hotteterre, J. M. Trio Sonatas Op. 2 Nos. 1 and 2. Schott.

Hottetere, J. M. Suite in / minor (H.M.). Bärenreiter.

Loeillet, J. B. Sonatas: Book I in A min; D min; G. Book II in B♭; g; c. Book III in E min; C min; A min. (H.M.). Bärenreiter.

Loeillet, J. B. Sonata, Op. 5 No. 1 in E. Musica Rara.

Loeillet, J. B. Trio Sonatas: No. 2 in F; No. 3 in D min; No. 6 in C min (H.M.). Bärenreiter.

Loeillet, J. B. Trio Sonata in F, Op. 1 (Fl. Ob. & Bc.). Schott.

Marcello, B. Sonatas in F, G, D min, G min. Peters.

Pepusch, J. C. 6 Trio Sonatas (Vn. on. Bc.). Breitkopf & Härtel.

Quantz, J. J. Sonata in D minor. Bärenreiter.

Quantz, J. J. Trio Sonata in G. Bärenreiter.

Schroeder, H. Trio Sonatas in F and C minor (H.M.). Bärenreiter.

Stoizel, G. H. Trio Sonata in F minor (N.M.A.). Bärenreiter.

Telemann, G. P. Sonatas in C min; F; G (H.M.). Bärenreiter.

Telemann, G. P. 6 Partitas in B♭, G, C min; G min; E min; E♭ (H.M.). Bärenreiter.

Telemann, G. P. Sonata und Spielstücke. Bärenreiter.

Telemann, G. P. Sonatas in G min, C minor. Bärenreiter.

Telemann, G. P. Sonata in G minor. Schott.

Telemann, G. P. Suite in G minor. Bärenreiter.

Telemann, G. P. Trio Sonata in D minor & E min (Fl. Ob. Bc.). Bärenreiter.

Tafelmusik I. – Quartet in G (Fl. Ob. Vn. Bc.). Bärenreiter.

Tafelmusik I. – Sonatas and Pieces from 'Der getrene Musik-meister' (H.M.). Bärenreiter.

Tafelmusik I. – Sonata in G (Ob. Vn. Bc.). Bärenreiter.

Tafelmusik II. – Trio Sonata (Fl. Ob. Bc.). Bärenreiter.

Tafelmusik II. – Trio Sonata in B♭. Bärenreiter.

Vivaldi, A. 'Il Pastor Fido' 6 Sonatas Op. 13 (ed. Upmeyer) in C; C; G; A; C; G (H.M.). Bärenreiter.

Vivaldi, A. Sonata in G minor. Bärenreiter.

Vivaldi, A. Sonata in C minor. Schott.

Vincent, T. Sonata in D. Schott.

Zelenka, J. D. Sonatas for 2 Oboes, Bc. (ed. Schoenbaum), No. 2, G min; No. 2, B♭; No. 4, G min; No. 5, F (H.M.). Bärenreiter.

Wind and Piano – 19th and 20th Centuries

The works in this category are generally more extrovert in character. They are popular with most audiences, sustaining an easy appeal and lightness of expression. Danzi is a firm favourite among wind players for his lucid melodies and exciting display. Lalliet inspires all that is most nostalgic in Victorian and Second Empire Europe – and in the best of taste.

Among the twentieth-century works, Goossens and Poulenc achieve a marvellous balance between coquetry and pastoral. Ton-That Tiêt is a Vietnamese composer who embraces Western techniques with an eye to the avant-garde.

Addison, J. Trio (Fl. Ob. Pno.). Augener.

Beethoven, L. van. Quintet Op. 16 (Ob. Cl. Bsn. Hn. Pno.). Musica Rara.

Bush, G. Trio (Ob. Bsn. Pno.). Novello.

Danzi, F. Quintet Op. 41 (Ob. Cl. Bsn. Hn. Pno.). Musica Rara.

Danzi, F. Quintet Op. 53 in F (Ob. Cl. Bsn. Hn. Pno.). Musica Rara.

Danzi, F. Quintet Op. 54 in D (Ob. Cl. Bsn. Hn. Pno.). Musica Rara.

Gal, H. Trio Op. 49 (Ob. Vc. Pno.). Osterriech.

Goossens, E. Patoral and Harlequinad (Fl. Ob. Pno.). Leduc.

Keller, G. Quintet in G minor (2 Fls. 2 Obs. Pno.). Schott.

Lalliet, T. Op. 22 Terzetto (Ob. Bsn. Pno.). Hamelle.

Lutyens, E. Music for Three Op. 65 (Fl. Ob. Pno.). Olivan (U.E.).

Mozart, W. A. Quintet in E♭, K. 452 (Ob. Cl. Bsn. Hn. Pno.). Bärenreiter.

Passini, E. Quintet (Fl. Ob. Cl. Bsn. Pno.). Transatlantique.

Poulenc, F. Trio (Ob. Bsn. Pno.). Hansen.

Rawsthorne, A. Sonatina for Fl. Ob. Pno.

Saint-Saëns, C. Caprice sur des Air Danois et Russe Op. 79 (Fl. Ob. Cl. Pno.). Durand.

Schmitt, F. A. Tour d'Anches Op. 97 (Ob. Cl. Bsn. Pno.). Durand.

Taffanel, P. Quintet (Fl. Ob. Cl. Bsn. Hn.). Leduc.

Tiêt, Ton-That. Tu Dai Ca'nh – Quatre Grands Paysages (Fl. Ob. Cl. Bsn. Pno.). Transatlantique.

Wind Quintets – Flute, Oboe, Clarinet, Bassoon, Horn

The String Quartet marks the highest point of musical art for string players. In the same way, the Wind Quintet has inspired the finest and most rewarding music in the wind ensemble repertoire. The consistency of inventiveness in all the works listed is proof in itself that the medium induces a special response from composers.

On the one hand we have colourful, zestful scores, such as Arnold's 'Sea Shanties' and Berio's 'Opus Number Zoo', both delightful entertainment for young and old alike: A.

Alternatively, there is the intense intellectualism of Stockhausen's 'Zeitmasze' and Schönberg's 'Quintet' – both prototypes for much of the music of a whole generation of composers: B.

Between these extremes lies that area of glorious musical art, indulging sharp contrasts of colour and mood (Hindemith, Barber) which form the backbone of a programme: C.

Although largely represented by the twentieth century, the Quintet had its devotees amongst eighteenth- and nineteenth-century composers such as Danzi and Reicha, who can certainly take praise for quantity, if not always for quality. Works marked (X) are technically very difficult and require intensive preparation.

When an extra clarinet is available to a quintet ensemble, Janacek's 'Mladi' (Youth) cannot be resisted for its freshness and vivid intensity of expression.

A Agay, D. Five Easy Dances. Presser.

C Arma, P. Sept Transparencies. Lemoine.

C Arnell, R. Cassation in 5 Parts (ed. L. Goossens). Peters.

A Arnold, M. Three Shanties. Paterson.

A Arrieu, C. Quintet in C major. Noël.

B Bainbridge, S. Quintet. U.M.P.

C Barber, S. Summer Music (X). Schirmer.

C Barthe, A. Aubade. Pinatel.

B Bedford, D. Pentomino. U.E.

C Bennett, R. R. Quintet. U.E.

A Berio, L. Opus Number Zoo – Child's Play with English, Italian and German words. U.E.

B Birtwistle, H. Refrains and Choruses (X). U.E.

C Bozza, E. 'Scherzo' and Variations sur un Thème Libre. U.M.P.

C Brod, H. Wind Quintet in B♭, Op. 2 No. 1. McGinnis.

C Cambini, G. G. Quintet No. 3 (ed. Josef Marx). McGinnis & Marx.

B Carter, E. Quintet (X). Ass. Music. Pub. N.Y.

C Chagrin, F. Divertimento. Augener.

C Chattelun, M. Suite Inchoative (Fl. C. A. Cl. Bsn. Hn.). Transatlantique.

C Colgrass, M. Quintet. M.C.A. (U.S.A.).

C Cooke, A. Quintet. Mills.

C Coral, G. Dialoghi (Fl. Ob. Cla. Hn. Tpt.). Zerboni.

A Damase, J. M. 17 Variations Op. 22. Leduc.

A Danzi, F. Quintet Op. 56 No. 1 in B♭. Leukhart.

A Danzi, F. Quintet Op. 56 No. 2 in G minor. Leukhart.

A Danzi, F. Quintet Op. 67 No. 1 in E min; No. 2 in E min; No. 2 in E♭. Kneusslin.

A Danzi, F. Quintet Op. 68 No. 2 in F. Peters.

A Danzi, F. Quintet Op. 68 No. 3 in D minor. Musica Rara.

A Danzi, F. Quintet Op. 86 No. 1 in A. Kneusslin.

A De Coursy, R. Fugue à la Rumba. BMI (Canada).

A Druschetzky. 4 Partitas. No. 9 in F; No. 10 in F; No. 13 in B♭; No. 21 in G (2 Obs. 2 Hns. Bsn.). Breitkopf & Härtel.

B Durkó, Z. Improvisations. P.W.M.

C Etler, A. Quintets No. 1 and 2. Schirmer.

C Fortner, W. 5 Bagatelles. Schott.

A Françaix, J. Quintet Op. 5. Eschig.

B Fricker, R. Quintet Op. 5 (X). Schott.

C Füssl. Kleine Kammermusik. Bärenreiter.

B Gentilucci, A. Diario II. Ricordi.

C Geuzmer. Quintet.

B Gerhard, R. Quintet (X). Mills.

C Heiden, E. Quintet. Schott.

C Helm, E. Quintet. Schott.

B Henze, H. W. Quintet. Schott.

C Hindemith, P. Kleine Kammermusik. Schott.

B Holliger, H. 'h' for wind quintet (X). Schott.

B Huber, K. 3 Movements in 2 Parts (Fl./Pic. Ob./C.A. Cl. Bsn. Hn.) (X). Bärenreiter.

C Karkoschka, E. Antinomie for W.Q. Breitkopf & Härtel.

C Kauffmann, L. J. Quintet. U.E.

B Kotoriski, W. Quintet. P.W.M.

B Krenek, E. 'Pentagramm' für Blasser. Bärenreiter.

C Lehmann, H. U. Episodes. Schott.

B Ligeti, G. Six Bagatelles (Ob. + Ob. d'am./C.A.) (X). Schott.

B Ligeti, G. Ten Pieces for Wind Quintet (X). Schott.

C Lutyens, E. Wind Quintet. Olivan (U.E.).

C Martinu, B. Four Madrigals. Eschig.

B Meale, R. Quintet. U.E.

A Milhaud, D. Suite d'Après Corette. Oiseau-Lyre.

B Milner, A. Quintet. Novello.

C Müller, P. Quintet. Musica Rara.

C Neilson, C. Quintet. Hansen.

C Panufnik, A. Quintet. Polish State Publishing House.

C Passini, E. Quintet. U.M.P.

C Patterson, P. Quintet. Weinberger.

C Perle, G. Quintet. Presser.

C Pierné, P. Op. 74 Suite Pittoresque. Leduc.

C Piston, W. Quintet. A.M.P.

A Reicha, A. Op. 88 No. 2 in E♭. Leukhart.

A Reicha, A. Op. 88 No. 3 in G. Artia.

A Reicha, A. Op. 88 No. 5 in B♭. Leukhart.

A Reicha, A. Op. 91 No. 1 in C. Kneusslin.

A Reicha, A. Op. 91 No. 3 in D. Kneusslin.
A Reicha, A. Op. 91 No. 5 in A. Breitkopf & Härtel.
A Reicha, A. Op. 91 No. 11. Artia.
A Reicha, A. Op. 100 No. 4 in E minor. Kneusslin.
A Reizenstein, F. Quintet. Boosey & Hawkes.
C Rieti, V. Quintet. Schirmer.
A Rosetti, A. Quintet (C.A.). Kneusslin.
A Rosetti, F. A. Quintet in E♭. Peters.
C Rota, N. Petite Offrande Musicale. Leduc.
B Roxburgh, E. Nebula II. U.M.P.
C Schilling, H. L. Zeacis Hafis – Quintet 67. Breitkopf & Härtel.
C Schmitt, F. Chants Alizes, Op. 125. Durand.
B Schönberg, A. Quintet Op. 26 (X). U.E.
C Schroeder. Divertimento. Peters.
C Schuller, G. Suite for Wind. McGinnis.
C Schuller, G. L. Quintet. Schirmer.
B Seiber, M. Permutazioni a Cinque. Schott.
B Stockhausen, K. Zeitmasze (Fl. Ob. C.A. Cla. Bsn.) (X). U.E.
B Stockhausen, K. Adieu (X). U.E.
C Stoker, R. Quintet. Peters.
C Szeligowski, R. Quintet. P.W.M.
C Villa-Lobos, H. Quintet. Eschig.
C Zender, H. Quintet Op. 3. Böte & Bock.

Sextets – Wind Quintet and Bass Clarinet

B Amy, G. Alpha-Beth. U.M.P.
C Janacek, L. Mladi (B.H.). Artia (Prague).

Wind Quartets – Flute, Oboe, Clarinet, Bassoon

B Babbitt, M. Woodwind Quartet. Schirmer.
C Baird, T. Divertimento.
B Bartolozzi, B. Concertazionia Quattro (X). Zerboni.
C Blacher, B. Divertimento. Schott.
C Bozza, E. Variants Op. 42. Leduc.

C Bozza, E. 3 Pièces Pour une Musique de Nuit. U.M.P.

B Carter, E. 8 Études and a Fantasy (X). A.M.P.

A Dittersdorf, K. D. von. 3 Partitas: No. 2 in F; No. 4 in A ;No. 20 in D (2 Obs. 2 Hns.). Breitkopf & Härtel.

A Françaix, J. Quartet. Schott.

A Stamitz, K. Quartet in E♭ (Ob. Cl. Bsn. Hn.). Leukhart.

C Villa-Lobos, H. Quartet. Eschig.

C Wellesz, E. Suite Op. 73 (Ob. Cl. Bsn. Hn.). Sikorski.

Wind Trios

C Arma, P. 3 Movements (Ob. Cl. Bsn.). U.M.P.

A Arrieu, C. Trio (Ob. Cl. Bsn.). U.M.P.

A Auric, G. Trio (Ob. Cl. Bsn.). Oiseau-Lyre.

C Blomdahl, K. B. Trio (Ob. Cl. Bsn.). F.S.T.

C Blumenthal. Trio (Fl. Ob. Bsn.). Peters.

A Bozza, E. Suite Brève en Trio (Ob. Cl. Bsn.). Leduc.

C Clementi, A. Triplum (Fl. Ob. Cl.). Zerboni.

A Françaix, J. Divertissement (Ob. Cl. Bsn.). Schott.

C Fortner, W. Serenade (Fl. Ob. Bsn.). Schott.

A Graun, K. H. Trios 1 and 2 in D and E (Ob. d'am. Bsn. Hn.). McGinnis.

C Graupner, C. Suite in F (2 Obs. 1 Fl.). Peters.

A Ibert, J. Cinq Pieces en Trio. Oiseau-Lyre.

A Jolivet, A. Pastorales de Noël (Fl. Ob. Bsn.). Heugel.

B Nilsson, B. 20 Gruppen (Pic. Ob. Cl.). U.E.

C Petrassi, G. Tre Per Sette (Fl. Ob. Cl.). Zerboni.

C Veress, S. Sonatina (Ob. Cl. Bsn.). Zerboni.

C Villa-Lobos, H. Trio (Ob. Cl. Bsn.). Eschig.

Oboe with String Ensembles

The combination of oboe and strings has a tradition of long association. Violins and oboes were born in modern form at about the same time in history, and thrived on a close musical partnership until the rise of the classical orchestra with Mozart, when woodwind became independent of the strings. The selection demonstrates a more lyrical response from composers.

Abel, C. F. Quartet Op. 12 No. 2 (Ob. Vn. Va. Vc.). Musica Rara.

Bach, J. C. Quartets Nos. 1, 3, 5 (Ob. Vn. Va. Vc.). Bärenreiter.

Bach, J. C. Quartet Op. 8 No. 2 (Ob. Vn. Va. Vc.). Musica Rara.

Bach, J. C. Quartet in C. Dunnebeil.

Bax, A. Quintet (Ob. Vlns. 1 & 2, Va. Vc.). Chappell.

Berkeley, L. Quartet (Ob. Vn. Va. Vc.). Chester.

Bliss, A. Quintet (Ob. Vns. 1 & 2 Va. Vc.). O.U.P.

Boccherini, L. Quintets Op. 21: No. 1 in D; No. 2 in C; No. 3 in D; No. 4 in B♭; No. 5 in G; No. 6 in E♭ (Ob. Vns. 1 & 2 Va. Vc.). Musica Rara.

Boccherini, L. Quintets Op. 45 Nos. 1, 2 and 3 (Ob. Vns. 1 & 2 Va. Vc.). Peters.

Boccherini, L. Quintets Op. 45 Nos. 4, 5 and 6 (Ob. Vns. 1 & 2 Va. Vc.). Sikorski.

Boccherini, L. Quintet in C (Fl. Ob. Vn. Va. Vc.). Musica Rara.

Britten, B. Phantasy Quartet, Op. 2 (Ob. Vn. Va. Vc.). Boosey & Hawkes.

Cruft, A. Fantasy Quartet (Ob. Vn. Va. Vc.). Williams.

Connolly, J. Triad III (Ob. Va. Cello). Novello.

Etler, A. Sextet (Ob. Cl. Bsn. Vn. Va. Vc.). Schirmer.

Gassmann, F. Quartet for Ob. Va. and 2 Vcs. Peters.

Giardini. Quartet in D, Op. 25, No. 3 (Ob. Vn. Va. Vc.). Breitkopf & Härtel.

Haydn, J. Sextet No. 14 (Ob. Bsn. Hn. Vn. Va. Vc.). Musica Rara.

Haydn, M. Divertimento in C minor (Ob. Va. Cl.). Doblinger.

Haydn, M. Divertimento in B minor (Ob. Bsn. Vn. Va. Cb.). Doblinger.

Jacob, G. Quartet (Ob. Vn. Va. Vc.). Novello.

Krommer (Kramár), F. Two Quartets (Ob. Vn. Va. Vc.). Artia

Le Fanu, N. Variations for Oboe and String Trio. Novello.

Milhaud, D. Les Rêves de Jacob (Ob. Vn. Va. Vc. Cb.). Heugel.

Milner, A. Quartet (Ob. Vn. Va. Vc.). Novello.

Mozart, W. A. Adagio (C.A. Vns. 1 & 2 Va. Vc.). Kasparek.

Mozart, W. A. Quartet K. 370 (Ob. Vn. Va. Vc.). Breitkopf & Härtel.

Penderecki, K. Capriccio per Oboe e II Archi. P.W.M.

Rainier, P. Quanta (Ob. Vn. Va. Vc.). Schott.

Reicha, A. Quintet. Simrock.

Roxburgh, E. Ecclissi (Ob. Vn. Va. Vc.). U.M.P.

Schroeder, H. Quartet (Ob. Vn. Va. Vc.). Schott.

Stamitz, C. Quartet Op. 8 No. 1 in D (H.M.) (Ob. Vn. Va. Vc.). Bärenreiter.

Stamitz, C. Quartet Op. 4 No. 6 in A (Ob. Vn. Va. Vc.). Leukhart.

Stamitz, C. Quartets Op. 8 No. 3 in E♭; Op. 8 No. 4 in E♭ (Ob. Vn. Va. Vc.). Musica Rara.

Stamitz, C. Quartet Op. 2 in D and A (Ob. Vn. Va. Vc.). McGinnis.

Telemann, G. P. Quartet in G (Ob. Fl. Vn. Bc.) (Tafelmusik I). Breitkopf & Härtel.

Vanhall, J. B. Quartet No. 7. Musica Rara.

Wordsworth, W. Quartet Op. 44. Lengnick.

Oboe Concertos with String Orchestra (S.O.) and Orchestra (O.)
(including concertante works)

The solo concerto repertoire is dominated by the eighteenth and twentieth centuries, Albinoni, Handel, Telemann and Vivaldi being the most prolific in the earlier period; Maderna taking the laurel more recently with no less than four works for solo oboe and orchestra. The Complete Works of Telemann, Handel and Mozart will be available eventually in Urtext form by Bärenreiter. These editions will be invaluable contributions to the player in search of an individually stylistic interpretation. Meanwhile, those recommended in the list provide excellent material for performance and study. Albinoni is served by a host of publishers, most of whom I have represented in the list.

In the twentieth-century works there is a wide range of idiom and style, from the pastoral ripples of Vaughan-Williams' folk tunes to the virtuosic brilliance of electronic colouring in Holliger's 'Siebengesang'. Maderna's 3rd Concerto requires an aptitude for improvisation together with an imaginative response to the material presented by the large orchestra. It is complex, but beautiful.

Ligeti's 'Doppelkonzert' is an exacting, high-ranging work, while Kotonski's 'Concerto' is more traditional in its demands. The cor anglais is presented as a concerto instrument with clarity and expressiveness in Piston's 'Fantasy'.

The nineteenth century, although limited in concerto works, shows brilliant colours in Hümmel's 'Introduction, Theme and Variations' for oboe; while Donizetti gives the cor anglais some exquisitely operatic treats in his 'Concertino'.

In concertante works Haydn and Mozart are complemented in the twentieth century by Blackwood, Dubois and Gyrowetz – not to forget a nineteenth-century contribution from Danzi.

The wide variety of styles and characteristics in all the concertos attests to the sometimes under-rated qualities of colour and projection of which the oboe and its family are capable.

Albinoni, T. Concerto Op. 7 No. 3 in B♭ (S.O.). Boosey & Hawkes.

Albinoni, T. Concerto Op. 7 No. 5 for 2 oboes (S.O.). Kneusslin.

Albinoni, T. Concerto Op. 7 No. 6 in D (S.O.). Boosey & Hawkes.

Albinoni, T. Concerto Op. 7 No. 9 in F minor (S.O.). Doblinger.

Albinoni, T. Concerto Op. 7 No. 12 in C minor (S.O.). Doblinger.

Albinoni, T. Concerto Op. 9 No. 2 (S.O.). Zerboni.

Albinoni, T. Concerto Op. 9 No. 3 (S.O.). Eulenberg.

Albinoni, T. Concerto Op. 9 No. 8 Concerto à 5 (S.O.). Musica Rara.

Albinoni, T. Concerto Op. 9 No. 9 for 2 oboes (S.O.). Ricordi.

Albinoni, T. Concerto Op. 9 No. 12 Concerto à 5 (S.O.). Musica Rara.

Alwyn, W. Concerto (O.). Lengnick.

Arnold, M. Concerto (O.). Paterson.

Bach, C. P. E. Concerto in B♭ (S.O.) Musikverlag. Rob Forberg.

Bach, J. C. Concerto in F (S.O.). Schott.

Bach, J. S. Concerto for Violin, Oboe and Strings. Peters.

Baguslowski, E. Concerto (Ob.-O.d'am.-C.A.-Musette) 1 player (O.). P.W.M.

Baird, T. Concerto (O.). Peters.

Bellini, V. Concerto in B♭. Ricordi.

Bellini, V. Concerto in E minor. Ricordi.

Benguerel, X. Musica per A Oboe-Conjunct de Camera. Moeck.

Besozzi, A. Concerto for Oboe and Strings. Musica Rara.

Blackwood, E. Concerto for 5 (Fl. Ob. Vn. Va. Vc.).) (O.). Schirmer.

Boughton, R. Concerto 1 (O.). Boosey & Hawkes.

Bush, G. Concerto (S.O.). Elkin.

Danzi, F. Sinfonia Concertante (Fl. Ob. Bn. Hn.). Musica Rara.

Dittersdorf, K. D. von. Concerto in G Major (S.O.). Breitkopf & Härtel.

Dittersdorf, K. D. von. Concerto in C Major (S.O.). Simrock.

Donizetti, G. Concertino (C.A.) (O.). Peters.

Dubois, P. M. Double Concerto (Ob. Bsn. Pno. Orch.). Leduc.

Eichner, E. Concerto in C (S.O.). O.U.P.

Eichner, E. Concerto in B♭ (S.O., Bc.). Hofmeister.

Endo, R. Ritsu (Oboe and Orchestra). Zerboni.

Fischer, J. C. Concerto in C. Augener.

Françaix, J. L'Horloge de Flore (O.). Transatlantique.

Genzmer. Kammerkonzert (S.). Schott.

Goossens, E. Concerto (O.). Leduc.

Gyrowetz, A. Sinfonia Concertante (Cl. Ob. Bn. Hn.). Musica Rara.

Hall, R. Three Idylls (S.O.). Hinrichsen.

Handel, G. F. Concertos in B♭ and G minor. Bärenreiter.

Haydn, J. Sinfonia Concertante (Ob. Bsn. Vn. Vc.). Breitkopf & Härtel.

Haydn, J. Concerto in C (Attributed to) (O.). Breitkopf & Härtel.

Henze, H. W. Double Concerto for Oboe and Harp (O.). Schott.

Hidas, F. Concerto (O.). E.M.B.

Holliger, H. Siebengesang (Ob. Orch. Singers Loudspeakers). Schott.

Holst, G. Fugal Concerto (Fl. Ob.) (S.O.). Novello.

Honegger, A. Concerto da Camera (Fl. C.A.) (S.O.). U.M.P. (Salabert).

Hummel, J. N. Introduction, Theme and Variations (O.). Musica Rara.

Ibert, J. Symphonie Concertante (S.O.). Leduc.

d'Indy, V. Fantasie (O.). Durand.

Jacob, G. Concertos 1 and 2 (S.O.). Williams.

Jacob, G. Rhapsody (C.A.) (S.O.). Williams.

Kotónsky, W. Concerto. P.W.M.

Krommer (Kramár), F. Concerto in F Op. 52. Artia.

Lamy, D. Nocturne (S.O. Hp. Tni.). Leduc.

Láng, I. Impulsioni (O.). Boosey & Hawkes.

Larsson, L. E. Concertino Op. 45 No. 2 (S.O.). Boosey & Hawkes.

Le Bouchet, M. Fantaisie Concertante (O.). De Lacour.

Lees, B. Concerto. Boosey & Hawkes.

Ligeti, G. Doppelkonzert (Fl. Ob.) (O.). Schott.

Lutyens, E. Concerto Grosso (Ob. Hp.) (S.O.). Chester.

Machonchy, E. Concerto (S.O.). Lengnick.

Maderna, B. Grand Aulodia (Fl. Ob.) (O.). Ricordi.

Maderna, B. Concerto 1.

Maderna, B. Concerto 2.

Maderna, B. Concerto 3 (O.). Salabert.

Marcello, B. Concerto in C min. Forberg.

Martin, F. Concerto for 7 Instruments (Fl. Ob. Cl. Bsn. Hn. Tpt. Tne.). U.E.

Martinu, B. Concerto (O.). Eschig.

Matej, J. Sonata for Oboe and Chamber Orchestra. Supraphon.

Milhaud, D. Concerto. Heugel.

Mozart, W. A. Concerto in C (O.). Boosey & Hawkes.

Mozart, W.· A. Symphony Concertante (Ob. Cl. Bsn. Hn.). Breitkopf & Härtel.

Novak, J. Concerto. Supraphon.

Pauer, J. Concerto for Oboe and Orchestra. Supraphon.

Piston, W. Fantasy (C.A.) (S.O.). A.M.P.

Platti, G. Konzert in G major. Schott.

Prestini, G. Concerto. Bongiovanni.

Rawsthorne, A. Concerto (S.O.). O.U.P.

Richter, F. Concerto in F (S.O.). Kneusslin.

Rivier, J. Concerto (S.O.). Transatlantique.

Rosetti, A. Concerto (on hire only). Brietkopf & Härtel.

Schroeder, H. Konzert (S.O.). Müller.

Schwenke, C. Concerto in C (S.O., Bc.). Hofmeister.

Skalkottas, N. Concertino. McGinnis.

Stamitz, C. Concerto in C minor (S.O., Bc.). Sikorski.

Stamitz, C. Concerto in B♭ (S.O., Bc.). Simrock.

Stölzel, G. H. Konzert in D (S.O., Bc.). Sikorsky.

Strauss, R. Concerto (O.). Breitkopf & Härtel.

Telemann, G. P. Concerto in E and D minor (S.O.). Sikorski.

Telemann, G. P. Concerto in E minor (S.O.). Sikorski.

Telemann, G. P. Concerto in F minor (S.O.). Peters.

Telemann, G. P. Concerto in C minor (S.O.). Schott.

Telemann, G. P. Concerto in G (Ob. d'Am.) (S.O.). Sikorski.

Telemann, G. P. Triple Concerto (Fl. Ob. d'Am. Va. d'Am.). Peters.

Telemann, G. P. Concerto Grosso in G minor (2 Obs.). Sikorski.

Telemann, G. P. Concerto (Alla Francese) in C (2 Obs.). Sikorski.

Vivaldi, A. (Complete Concertos). Ricordi.

Vaughan-Williams, R. Concerto (S.O.). O.U.P.
Veress, S. Passacaglia Concertante (S.O.). Zerboni.
Zimmerman, B. A. Konzert für Oboe und Kleinorchester. Schott.
Zach, J. Concerto (S.O.).

Miscellaneous

Most of the works in this category are twentieth-century. Before Schönberg's 'Pierrot Lunaire' was composed in 1912 it was the exception rather than the rule for composers to write music for any but standard combinations. Nevertheless, I have included works by Beethoven and Vogt for Trios of two Oboes and Cor Anglais because this medium is most adaptable to the more variegated ensembles of twentieth-century chamber music.

At the other end of the scale there is Hindemith's Trio, Op. 47, for the very unlikely combination of Piano, Viola and Heckelphone. In general, composers have not been too kind to the bass instrument of the family. Hindemith is an exception. By combining the voluptuous tone of the viola with the heckelphone he acknowledges its true expressive richness.

There is a blissful no-man's land about most of these pieces which makes them marry happily with chamber music of any period or style in music history.

Abbado, M. 'Quindici Poesie T'ang' (Mezzo Sop. Fl. Ob. Vc. Pf.). Zerboni.
Antonion, T. Synthesis (for Ob. Perc. Hammond Org. Cb.). Bärenreiter.
Bach, J. C. Sextet in C (Ob. 2 Hns. Vn. Vc. Bc.). Musica Rara.
Badings, H. Trio 4a (2 Obs. C.A.). Donemus.
Bartolozzi, B. Concertazioni per Oboe e Alcum Strumenti (Ob. Va. Guit. Cb. 1 Perc. ad. lib.). Zerboni.
Beethoven, L. van. Trio Op. 87 (2 Obs. C.A.). Peters.

Beethoven, L. van. Variations on 'La ci darem la mano' (2 Obs. C.A.). Breitkopf & Härtel.

Birtwistle, H. Death and Nick's Love Song (3 C.A. Hp.). U.E.

Boismortier. 3 Concertos for 5 Oboes. Breitkopf & Härtel.

Boismortier. 6 Sonatas Op. 7 (3 Obs.). Schott.

Carter, E. Sonata (Fl. Ob. Vc. H'cd.). A.M.P.

Chou, Wen-Chung. Suite for Wind Quartet & Harp. Peters.

Dodgson, S. Suite in D (Ob. Hp.). O.U.P.

Dubois, P. M. Lou Cascarelet, dançes provençale (Tamb. ad lib.) (3 Obs.). U.M.P.

Endo, R. Dessein Improvisation (Fl. Ob. Pno. Perc.). Zerboni.

Endo, R. Wandering Flames (Ob. Cl. Pno.). Zerboni.

Fricker, P. R. 5 Canons for 2 Fls. 2 Obs.

Gow, D. Quartet Op. 28 (Fl. Ob. Vc. H'chord). Musica Rara.

Halffter, C. Antiphonismoi für sieben spieler (Fl. (+Al. Fl.) Ob. (+C.A.) Cl. Pno. Vn. Va. Vc.). U.E.

Haydn, J. Divertimento in F (2 Obs. 2 Hns. 2 Bsns.). Musica Rara.

Haydn, J. March in G (2 Obs. 2 Hns. 2 Bsns.). Musica Rara.

Haydn, M. Divertimento in D min. (2 Obs. 2 Hns. 2 Bsns.). Doblinger.

Hindemith, P. Trio Op. 47 (Vla. Heckelphone, Pno.). Schott.

Holliger, H. Vier Miniaturen (Sop. Ob. d'Am. Celesta Hp.). Schott.

Holliger, H. Mobile (Ob. Hp.). Schott.

Holliger, H. Trio (Ob. (+C.A.) Va. Hp.). Ars Viva Verlag, Mainz.

Holst, G. Terzetto (Fl. Ob. Va.). Chester.

Jacob, G. 2 Pieces for 2 Oboes, 1 Cor Anglais. Williams.

Jelinek, A. Cor Anglais Sonata A Tre Op. 15 No. 7 (Ob. C.A. Bn.). U.E.

Jolivet, A. Controversia (Ob. Hp.). Billandot.

Lahnsen, C. Kleine Pfeifermusik für 2 Oboes. Breitkopf & Härtel.

Lampersberg, G. Musik für Oboe und 13 Instruments (Vn.

Va. Vc. Cb. B-Cl. Bsn. Hn. Tpt. Tne. kleine trommel. Hp.
Celesta. Pno.). U.E.
Lehmann, H. U. Spiele für Oboe und Harp. Schott.
Maderna, B. Aulodia per Lotha (Ob. d'Am. guit.). Zerboni.
Malige, F. 6 Inventions for 2 Oboes. Breitkopf & Härtel.
Martinu, B. Quartet (Ob. Vn. Vc. Pno.). Eschig.
Moser, F. J. Trio in C Op. 38 (2 Obs. C.A.). Bosworth.
Musgrave, T. Impromptu (Ob. Fl.). Chester.
Pinkham, D. Variations for Oboe and Organ. Peters.
Pla, J. B. Sechs Sonata (2 Obs.). Schott.
Roesgen-Champion, M. Deuxieme Nocturne. Leduc.
Schroeder, H. Concertina (Vn. Ob. Organ). Schott.
Singer, L. Musica a Due (Ob. Guit.). Zerboni.
Schweizer, K. Chamber Music (Fl. C.A. Vn. Vc. H'cd.).
Bärenreiter.
Vogt. Andante Religioso (2 Obs. C.A.). Castallat.
Weichlein, R. Duets (2 Obs.). Breitkopf & Härtel.
Wyttenbach, J. Drei Sätz (Ob. Hp. Pno.). Schott.
Yun, I. Trio (Fl. Ob. Vn.).
Zimmerman, H. Trios 1 and 2 (Ob. Bsn. Vc.). Schmidt.

Some Important Tutors and Instruction Manuals

A. 17th–18th Centuries
Banister, J. The Sprightly Companion. London, 1695.
Freillon Poncein, J.-P. La Veritáble Manière B'Apprendre à Jouer en Perfection du Hautbois. Paris, 1700.
Hotteterre, J. Principes de la Flute Traversiere, de la Flute-a-bec et du Haut-bois. Paris, 1707. (English translation by D. Losocki, London, 1968.)
Talbot, J. Music Manuscript 1187, Christ Church, Oxford. c. 1700.
Fischer, J. C. (Attributed to). New and Compleat Instructions for the Hoboy. Cahusac, London, 1790.

B. 19th Century
Barret, A. M.-R. A Complete Method for the Oboe. London, 1850. Enlarged 2nd edition 1862.

Brod, H. Grande Methode. Paris, c. 1835.
Garnier, F. J. Methode de Hautbois. Paris, 1800.
Hinke, G. Praktische Elementarschule. Leipzig, 1888.
Kling, H. Grifftabelle fur Oboe. Berlin, 1894.
Langey, O. Tutor for the Oboe. Berlin, 1894.
Mariani, G. Metodo Popolare P. Oboe. Milan, c. 1900.
Marco, E. Metodo de Oboe. Madrid, 1870.
Sellner, J. Oboeschule. Vienna, 1825.
Vogt, A.-G. Methode. Paris, c. 1812.

C. 20th Century

Bartolozzi, B. New Sounds for Woodwind (edited by R. Smith-Brindle). London, 1967.
Gillet, F. Methode Pour le Debut du Hautbois. Paris, 1940.
Mazarov, N. Shkola Alia Goboya, Vol. I. Moscow, 1939. Vol. II. 1941.
Pietzsch, G. Schule fur Oboe. Leipzig, 1911.
Marx, J. A Methodical Study of the Oboe. 5 Vols.
Rothwell, E. Oboe Technique (new edition). London, 1974.
Sprenkle, R. and Ledet, D. The Art of Oboe Playing. Illinois, 1961.
Singer, S. Methode Complete pour le Hautbois. Warsaw, 1913.

Selected Studies for the Modern Oboe

Bozza, E. 14 Studies in Karnatic Modes. Leduc.
Bozza, E. 18 Etudes. Leduc.
Brown, J. 370 Exercises. Leduc.
Braun, C. 18 Caprices. Breitkopf & Härtel.
Ferling, C. 144 Studies and Preludes, Vols I & II. Breitkopf & Härtel.
Hofmann, R. 10 Melodic Exercises and Pieces Op. 58. Breitkopf & Härtel.
Gillet, F. Etudes Pour l'Enseignement Superieur du Hautbois. Leduc.
Karg-Elert. Etuden-Schule Op. 41. Breitkopf & Härtel.
Luft. 24 Studies.

Socewicz, W. Scales, Arpeggios and Intervals. P.W.M.
Snieckowski, S. Selected Studies Bks I–III. P.W.M.

Orchestral Studies

Bach, J. S. Complete Arias (Masses, Oratorios, Cantatas)
for Sop. Alto, Ten, Bass: Oboe and Continuo. Musica Rara.
Bach, J. S. Bach Studies: Vols I & II (Heinze). Breitkopf &
Härtel.
Bach, J. S. Difficult Passages for Oboe, Ob. d'Am., C.A.
(Rothwell). Boosey & Hawkes.
Brahms, J. Orchesterstudien (9). Hofmeister.
Crozzoli, S. Passi Difficile e 'A Solo' (Ob. & C.A.) in 3
volumes (Italian Operas). Ricordi.
Faldi. 12 Brevi Studi Seriali.
Handel, G. F. Studies in 4 Volumes (Heinze). Concerti,
Occasional Music, Oratorios, etc. Breitkopf & Härtel.
Heinze. Orchestral Studies, Vols I & II. Breitkopf & Härtel.
Hofmeister. Orchestral Studies (C.A.). Breitkopf & Härtel.
Nagy, S. Orchestral Extracts.
Rothwell, E. Orchestral Studies; Difficult Passages Ob. &
C.A. 3 Volumes. Boosey & Hawkes.
Strauss, R. Orchestral Studies for Oboe and C.A. 2 Volumes
(Vol. II with ob. d'am. also). Peters.
(Various). Traites Difficiles for Oboe and Cor Anglais. Leduc.
Wagner. (ed. Gerlach). Hofmeister.

Appendix III

Fingering charts

o = open
● = closed
◐ = half-closed or plate only on L.H.1

hollow, covered sound.

soft, distant sound.

horn-like and resonant.

mellow and muted.

✳ On thumb-plate models the first finger right hand
need not be used for B♭ and C.

well-tuned, sweet quality.

slightly flat, muted sound.

rich, woody quality.

mellow.

small, quiet quality.

mellow, but rich (slightly flat), not tempered by lip.

brilliant.

❋ = Harmonic

213

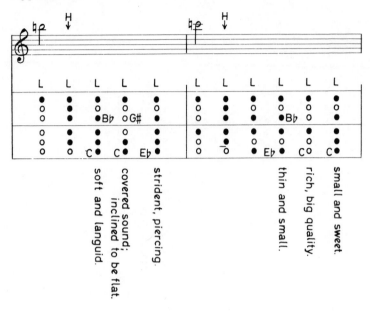

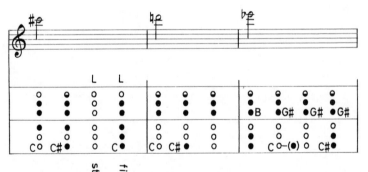

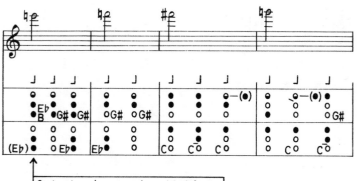

3rd octave key may be added from
here to the highest note of the chart.

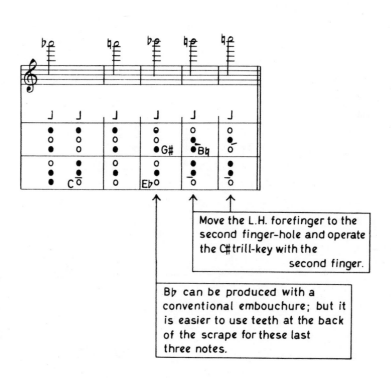

Move the L.H. forefinger to the
second finger-hole and operate
the C♯ trill-key with the
second finger.

B♭ can be produced with a
conventional embouchure; but it
is easier to use teeth at the back
of the scrape for these last
three notes.

Brief Bibliography

Sources Consulted

Anderson, E. *The Letters of Mozart and his Family*, London 1938.

Aristotle. *De Audibus.*

Bach, C. P. E. *Versuch über die wahre Art das Klavier zu spielen* (1753 and 1762). *Essay on the True Art of the Keyboard*, Eng. Trans.: W. J. Mitchell, 1949.

Baines, A. *Woodwind Instruments and their History* (3rd Edn.), London 1967.

Banister, J. *The Sprightly Companion*, London 1695.

Bartolozzi, B. *New Sounds for Woodwind* (Ed.: R. Smith-Brindle), London 1967.

Bate, P. A. T. *The Oboe* (3rd Edn.), London 1975.

Berlioz, H. *Les Soirées de l'Orchestre* (1852). *Evenings in the Orchestra*, Eng. Trans.: C. R. Fortescue.

Berlioz, H. *Traité de l'instrumentation*, Paris 1845.

Burney, C. *A General History of Music from the earliest ages to the present period* (1789). Modern Edn.: Dover Publications, New York 1957.

Carse, A. *The Orchestra from Beethoven to Berlioz*, Cambridge 1948.

Carse, A. *The Orchestra in the 18th century*, Cambridge 1940.

Couperin, F. *L'Art de Toucher le Clavecin*, Paris 1717. Reprinted in Eng. trans. Leipzig 1933.

Dart, T. *The Interpretation of Music* (4th Edn.), London 1967.

Dolmetsch, N. *The Viol.*

Donington, R. *The Interpretation of Early Music.* New version, London 1974.

Einstein, A. *Mozart, His Character, His Work*, London 1946.

Encyclopaedia Britannica. Oboe, Cor Anglais, by K. Schlesinger, 11th Edn. 1910.

Grove, G. *Dictionary of Music and Musicians:* 'The Oboe', by E. Halfpenny and P. A. T. Bate (5th Edn.), 1954.

Hanslick, E. *Music Criticisms 1846–99,* Eng. trans.: H. Pleasants. Revised Edn., London 1963.

Hawkins, J. *General History of the Science and Practice of Music,* London 1776.

Helmholtz. *On the Sensations of Tone,* Eng. trans.: Ellis, 1875.

Homer. *The Iliad.*

Hotteterre, J. *Principes de la Flute Traverse, de la Flute a bec, et du Haut-bois,* Paris 1707. *Principles of the Flute, Recorder and Oboe,* trans.: D. Lasocki, London 1968.

Mattheson, J. *Das neu-eröffnete Orchestre,* Hamburg 1713.

Marx, J. *The Tone of the Baroque Oboe* (Galpin Society Journal IV, 1951), London.

Musical World. London 1838.

Nietsche. *Ecce Homo.* Eng. trans.: W. Kaufmann, New York 1969.

Praetorius, M. *Syntagma Musicum,* 1619. Eng. trans.: H. Blumen, Bärenreiter 1949.

Prelleur, P. *The Modern Music Master,* London 1731. Facsimile reprint edited by H. Hyatt King in the series 'Documenta musicalogica', Bärenreiter.

Quantz, J. J. *Versuch einer Anweisung die Flöte traversiere zu spielen.* Eng. trans.: E. R. Reilly, London 1966.

Raguenet, F. *Parallèle des Italiens et des François,* 1702. Eng. trans. in Strunk, 1951.

Reichardt, J. F. *Briefe gerschrieben auf einer Reise nach Wien,* 1810. Eng. trans. in Strunk, 1951.

Sachs, C. *History of Musical Instruments,* New York 1940.

Schlesinger, K. *The Greek Aulos,* London 1939.

Schopenhauer. *Die Welt als Wille und Vorstellung,* Dresden 1818.

Sprenkle, R., and Ledet, D. *The Art of Oboe Playing,* Illinois 1961.

Statius. *Thebaid, VI* (120–121).

Strunk, O. *Source Readings in Music History,* New York 1951.

Talbot, J. *Music MS. 1187*, Christ Church, Oxford, c. 1700.
Wagner, R. *Preface* to 'Tristan und Isolde'.
Woolley, L. *History Unearthed*, London 1958.
Wynne, B. *Music in the Wind*, London 1967.

Further Reading
Early History

Aristoxenus. *Harmonic Elements* (Eng. trans. in Strunk), re aulos tuning and intonation.
Plutarch. *De Musica*.
Plato. *The Republic*.

Eighteenth century interpretations

Arnold, F. T. *The Art of Accompaniment from a Thorough-bass*, 1931.
Avison, C. *An Essay on Musical Expression*, 1752.
Dannreuther, E. *Musical Ornamentation*, 1893.
Dolmetsch, A. *The Interpretation of the Music of the XVIIth and XVIIIth Centuries*, 1915.
Galpin, F. W. *Old English Instruments of Music*, London 1965. *Galpin Society Journal*, London.
Hailperin, P. *Some Technical Remarks on the Shawm and Baroque Oboe*, Basel 1970.
Landon, H. C. Robbins. *The Symphonies of Josef Haydn*, London 1955.
Muffat. *Auserlesene Instrumental-Music*, 1701.
Purcell, H. *Preface* to *A Choice Collection of Lessons*. Reprinted, London 1895 (Purcell Society).
Terry, C. S. *Bach's Orchestra*, London 1932.

General

Baines, A. (ed.). *Musical Instruments through the Ages*, London 1966.
Carse, A. *Musical Wind Instruments*, London 1939.
Donington, R. *The Instruments of Music*, London 1949.
Fétis, F. J. *Biolgraphie Universelle des Musiciens*, Paris 1868.
Galpin, F. W. *European Musical Instruments*, London 1937.
Langwill, L. G. *Index of Musical Wind-Instrument Makers*, 3rd Edn., Edinburgh 1972.

Nederveen, C. J. *Acoustical Aspects of Woodwind Instruments*, Amsterdam 1969.

Parke, W. *Musical Memoirs*, London 1830.

Prestini, G. *Notizie intorno alla storia degli strumenti*, Bologna 1925.

Risatti, H. *New Music Vocabulary*. A guide to notational signs for contemporary music. Illinois 1976.

Sachs, C. *Rhythm and Tempo*, New York 1953.

Serr, W. *The New World of Electronic Music*, New York 1972.

Wood, A. *The Physics of Music*, London 1944.

Discography

Solo Oboe

BERIO, Luciano
Sequenza VII
    Holliger   Philips 6500 631

BRITTEN, Benjamin
Six Metamorphoses after Ovid, Op. 49
    Francis   Saga ARC13*
    Hanus   Supraphon SUAST50906*
    Francis   Argo ZRG842*
    Gomberg   Van. C-10064

CASTIGLIONI, Niccolo
Alef
    Holliger   Philips 6500 202*

STOCKHAUSEN, Karlheinz
Spiral
    Holliger   DG2612 023*

Oboe and Piano

HINDEMITH, Paul
Sonata (1938)
    Jaeger, True   Mark 25726*
    Roseman   Desto 6484

KŘENEK, Ernst
Four Pieces
    Holliger, Wyttenbach   Philips 6500 202*

NIELSEN, Carl
Fantasy Pieces, Op. 2
    Lucarelli, Lebon   Lyrichord LLST 7155*

Note: Entries followed by an asterisk (*) are not currently available. Wind Quartet and Wind Quintet are indicated by wq. Woodwind Ensemble is indicated by ww ens.

The Oboe

POULENC, Francis
Sonata (1962)
    Pierlot, Fevrier   Nonesuch 71033
    Borgue, Fevrier   EMI EMSP 553*

SCHUMANN, Robert
Romances (3), Op. 94
    Goossens, Moore   HMV HQM 1087*
    Roseman   Desto 6484

Trios and Quartets for Wind

ARNOLD, Malcolm
Trio, Op. 37 (fl ob cl)
    Czech Philharmonic wq   Supraphon SUAST50582*

AURIC, Georges
Trio (1938) **(ob cl bsn)**
    Adelstein, Listokin, Popkin   GC S-4076

CARTER, Elliot
Eight Etudes and a Fantasy (1950)
    Dorian wq   Can. 31016

FRANÇAIX, Jean
Divertissement (1947) **(ob cl bsn)**
    Melos   Ang. S-36586
    Philadelphia ww ens.   CSP AMS-6213

STAMITZ, Karl
Quartet, Op. 8, No. 2 (ob cl hn bsn)
    Koch, Leister, Pusek, Seifert   DG2530 077*
    Czech Wind   Supraphon 111 1082*

Wind Quintets

ARNOLD, Malcolm
Three Shanties
    London wq   Argo 5326

BARBER, Samuel
Summer Music, Op. 31 (1956)
    New York wq   Con.-Disc. 216

BIRTWISTLE, Harrison
Refrains and Choruses
    Danzi wq   Philips SAL3669*

BOZZA, Eugene
Variations, Op. 40
    Copenhagen wq   Decca LXT2803*

CARTER, Elliot
Quintet (1949)
    Dorian wq   Can. 31016

DAMASE, Jean-Michel
Variations, Op. 22 (1950)
    French wq   Osieau Lyre OL50122*

DANZI, Franz
Quintet in B flat, Op. 56, No. 1
Quintet in G minor, Op. 56, No. 2
    French wq   Ducretet Thomson DL53005*
    Haifa wq   Pye GSGC14034*
    New York wq   Nonesuch 71108
Quintet in E minor, Op. 67, No. 2
    Haifa wq   Pye GSGC14034*
    New York wq   Nonesuch 71108

ETLER, Alvin
Quintet (1955)
    New York wq   Con.-Disc. 216

FRICKER, Peter Racine
Quintet, Op. 5
    London wq   Argo 5326

GERHARD, Roberto
Quintet (1928)
    London wq   Argo 5326

HENZE, Hans Werner
Quintet (1953)
    Dorian wq   Can. 31016

HINDEMITH, Paul
Kleine Kammermusik, Op. 24, No. 2
    Haifa wq   Pye GSGC14034*
    Czech Philharmonic wq   Supraphon SUAST50431*
    Oberlin Faculty wq   Coro. S-1408

HOLMBOE, Vagn
Notturno, Op. 19 (1940)
    Danish wq   Philips 6578 005*
    Goteborg wq   BIS LP24*

LIGETI, György
Ten Pieces
    Stockholm wq   HMV E 061-34091*

LUTYENS, Elizabeth
Quintet
    Leonardo wq   Argo 5425

The Oboe

MATHIAS, William
Quintet, Op. 22
    Nash Ensemble   Argo ZRG771*

NIELSEN, Carl
Quintet, Op. 43 (1922)
Danish wq	HMV DB5200-03*
Copenhagen wq	Decca LXT2803*
Philadelphia wq	CBS SBRG72133*
Melos Ensemble	HMV ASD2438*
Danish wq	Philips 6578 0001*
Lark wq	Lyrichord 7155
Vestjysk Ch. Ens.	DG 2530515

ROSENBERG, Hilding
Quintet (1959)
    Stockholm wq   HMV E055 34629*

SCHÖNBERG, Arnold
Quintet, Op. 26
Danzi wq	Philips SAL3669*
N.E. Cons. Ch. Pl.	GC/NEC 102

SEIBER, Matyás
Permutazioni à cinque
    London wq   Argo 5326

STOCKHAUSEN, Karlheinz
Zeitmasse
    Cond. Boulez   Odyssey 32160154

VILLA-LOBOS, Heitor
Quintette en forme de Choros (1928, rev. 1953)
New Art wind	Nixa WLP5360*
Stockholm wq	HMV E 061-34091*
Soni Ventorum wq	Lyrichord 7168

Wind Sextet

JANÁČEK, Leoš
Sextet for Wind Instruments, Mládi (Youth)
Philadelphia wq	Philips ABR4057*
Melos Ensemble	HMV ASD2344*
Prague wq	Supraphon 111 1177*
Foerster wq	Panton 11 0214*
Rudel, cond.	Desto 6428

Oboe and Strings

BAX, Arnold
Quintet (1923)
    Goossens/International String Quartet   NGS76-77*

BLISS, Arthur
  Quintet (1927)
    Goossens, Melos Ensemble   HMV HQS1299*
    Graeme, Melos Ensemble   Ev. 3135

BRITTEN, Benjamin
  Phantasy Quartet, Op. 2 (1932) **(or Fantasy for Oboe and Strings)**
    Gomberg/Galimir Trio   Esoteric ES504*
    Hanus/Janáček Quartet   Supraphon SUAST50960*
    Francis, Hurwitz   Argo ZRG842*
    Gomberg, Raimondi, Zaslav, Stuch   Van. C-10064

MOZART, Wolfgang Amadeus
  Quartet in F, K370
    Goossens/Lener Trio   Columbia LX256-7*
    Gomberg, Galimir   Van. C-10064
    Winschermann/Kehr Trio   Telefunken LGX66065*
    Koch/Berlin Philharmonic Ensemble   DG138996
    Sous/Endres Quartet   Turnabout 34035
    Wilson, Gabrieli   Classics for Pleasure CFP121*
    Boston Symphony Chamber Players   RCA LSB4014*

RAINIER, Priaulx
  Quanta (1962)
    London Oboe Quartet   Argo ZRG660*

TELEMANN, Georg Philipp
  Quartet in G (Tafelmusik I)
    Concerto Amsterdam/Bruggen
            Das Alte Werk SAWT9449-50*

Concertos

ALBINONI, Tommaso
  12 Concertos, Op. 7
    Pierlot/I Solisti Veneti/cond. Scimone   Erato STU70883*
  Concertos, Op. 7, Nos. 3, 6, 9, 12
    Pierlot/L'Ensemble Orchestral de l'Oiseau Lyre/cond. Froment   Oiseau Lyre OLS120*
  Concertos, Op. 7, Nos. 3, 6
    Nepalov/Moscow CO/cond. Barshai   West 8323
  Concerto in D minor, Op. 9, No. 2
    Evert van Tright/I Musici   Philips SABL158*
    Holliger/I Musici   Philips 6747 041*
    Pierlot, Scimone/Soloisti Veneti   RCA VICS-1691
  Concerto in F for two oboes, Op. 9, No. 3
    Holliger, Bourgue/I Musici   Philips 6580 001*
  Concerto in C, Op. 9, No. 4
    Winschermann/Deutsche Bach Solisten   Nonesuch 71148

The Oboe

Concerto in G minor Op. 9, No. 3
Driehuys/I Musici   Philips 6580 001*

BACH, Carl Philipp Emmanuel
Concerto in B flat W. 165
Holliger, Auberson/Geneva Bar. Orch   Mon. S-2088
Concerto in E flat, W. 164
Holliger/ECO/cond. Leppard   Philips 6500 830

BACH, Johann Sebastian
Concerto for violin, oboe, and strings, S. 1060
Grumiaux, Holliger/NPO/cond. De Waart   Philips 6500 119
Menuhin, Goossens/Bath Festival/cond. Menuhin
  Ang. S-36103
Driehuys, Michelucchi/I Musici   Philips 6580 067*
Perlman, Black/ECO/cond. Berenboim   Ang. S-37076
Kaine, Miller/St. Martin-in-the-Fields/cond. Marriner
  Argo ZRG-820; -820

Concerto in A major (arr. oboe d'amore by Tovey)
Goossens/Philharmonia Orchestra/cond. Susskind
  HMV HQM1087*

Concerto in F for oboe (arr. Töttcher and Muller)
Holliger, A. Milhaud/Orch. Ch. Romond   Mon. S-2091

BELLINI, Vincenzo
Concertino in C
Lord/Academy/cond. Marriner   SOL277*
Concerto in E flat for oboe and orchestra
Lord/Academy/cond. Marriner   Oiseau Lyre S-277

CIMAROSA, Domenico
Concerto[1]
Goossens/Liverpool PO/cond. Sargent   HMV CLP1698*
Holliger, Maag/Bamberg Sym.   OG139152

ELGAR, Edward
Soliloquy[2]
Goossens/Bournemouth Sinfonietta/cond. Del Mar
  RCA LRL1 5133*

FRANÇAIX, Jean
L'Horloge de Flore
de Lancie/LSO/cond. Previn   RCA LSB4094*

---

[1] As composed, not truly a concerto, and not for oboe, but a suite of three pieces arranged for oboe and strings by Arthur Benjamin.
[2] Elgar, having heard Goossens play in the *Froissart* overture, wrote the *Soliloquy*, which was intended as a part of a suite, but never completed the work or scored this movement. Scored in 1967 by Gordon Jacob, it was recorded in 1976 by Goossens.

226

GOOSSENS, Eugene
Concerto in one movement
Goossens/Philharmonia Orch./cond. Susskind
Columbia DCX84-85*

HANDEL, George Frederic
Concertos (No. 1 in B flat; No. 2 in B flat; No. 3 in G minor)
Goossens/Bath Festival Orch./cond. Menuhin Ang. S-36103
Lord/Academy of St. Martin-in-the-Fields/cond. Marriner
Argo 5442
Holliger/ECO/cond. Leppard   Philips 6500 240*
Craxton/Collegium Musicum Londinii/cond. Michington
Saga 5236*
(No. 1 only:)
Rothwell/Halle Orch./cond. Barbirolli   Pye GSGC14086*

HAYDN, Joseph
Concerto in C major
Hantak/Prague SO/cond. Newstone
Supraphon SUA50377*
Milde/Pro Musica Stuttgart/cond. Reinhardt
Turnabout 34031
Kalmus/Munich Ch. Orch./cond. Stadlmeyer   DG135069*
Sinfonia Concertante in B flat, Op. 84
soli/ECO/cond. Barenboim   Ang. S-36582
soli/Philharmonia Hungarica/cond. Dorati
6-London STS-15229134
soli/Vienna Philharmonic/cond. Böhm   DG2530398

HENZE, Hans Werner
Double concerto for oboe, harp, and strings
H. Holliger, U. Holliger/Zürich Collegium Musicum/cond.
Sacher   DG139 396*

HOLLIGER, Heinz
Siebengesang
Holliger/Basel CO/cond. Travis   DG2530 318*

HOLST, Gustav
Fugal Concerto
Bennett, Graeme/ECO/cond. Imogen Holst Lyrita SRCS34*

HONEGGER, Arthur
Concerto da camera
Solum, Camden/Eng. Sinfonia/cond. Dilkes
EMI EMDS5526*

IBERT, Jacques
Sinfonia concertante
de Lancie/LSO/cond. Previn   RCA LSB4094*

227

The Oboe

KROMMEŘ-KRAMÁR, František
Concerto, Op. 57
    Duchon/Prague SO/cond. Neumann
        Supraphon Musica Antiqua Bohemica 19371*

LIGETI, György
Double Concerto
    Nicolet, Holliger/London Sinfonietta/cond. Atherton
        Decca HEAD12*

MARCELLO, Alessandro
Concerto in C minor
    Goossens/Philharmonia Orch./cond. Susskind
        HMV HMQ1087*
    Pierlot/Orchestre de l'Oiseau Lyre/cond. Froment
        Oiseau Lyre OLS106*
    Rothwell/orch. cond. Barbirolli   Pye GSGC14142*
(in original D minor form:)
    Holliger/Dresden Staatskapelle/cond. Negri
        Philips 6500 413

MARTIN, Frank
Concerto for seven instruments
    Orchestre de la Suisse Romande/cond. Ansermet
        Decca ECS578*
    Chicago SO/cond. Martinon   RCA SB6710*

MARTINŮ, Bohuslav
Concerto (1955)
    Hantak/Brno PO/cond. Turnovsky
        Supraphon SUAST50486*

MILHAUD, Darius
Concerto (1957)
    Vandeville/ORTF Orch./cond. Suzan
        Barclay Inédit 995 032*

MOZART, Wolfgang Amadeus
Concerto in C, K314
    de Lancie/Philadelphia Orch./cond. Ormandy
        Columbia M3-6452
    Holliger/NPO/cond. De Waart   Philips 6500 174
    Koch/Berlin PO/cond. Karajan   3-Ang. S-3783
    Black/Academy of St. Martin-in-the-Fields/cond. Marriner
        Philips 6500 379
    Truetschek/Vienna PO/cond. Böhm   DG2530257
Sinfonia concertante in E flat, K297b
    soli/ECO/cond. Barenboim   Ang. S-36582
    soli/Berlin PO/cond. Karajan   3-Ang. S-3783
    soli/Vienna PO/cond. Böhm   DG 139156
    Academy of St. Martin/cond. Marriner   Philips 6500 380

soli/Berlin PO/cond. Prince Konoye   Columbia LX661-4S*

STRAUSS, Richard
Oboe Concerto in D
Goossens/Philharmonia Orch./cond. Galliera
HMV CLP1698*
Holliger/New Philharmonia Orch./cond. De Waart
Philips 6500 174
Koch/Berlin PO/cond. Karajan   DG 2530439

TELEMANN, Georg Philipp
Concerto in C minor
Koch/Hamburg Telemann Soc./cond. Böttcher   DG135 080*
Concerto for three oboes and three violins in B flat
Emil Seiler Chamber Group   DG135 080*
Concerto in G major for oboe d'amore and strings
Holliger/Dresden Staatskapelle/cond. Negri
Philips 6500 413
Overture in C for three oboes, strings, and continuo
Winschermann, Bolz, Trenz/Saar Orch./cond. Ristenpart
Nonesuch 71132
Concerto in F minor
Telemann Soc./cond. Schulze   Vox DL590*
Wolsing/Danish Radio Orch./cond. Wöldike
Columbia LDX2*
Nepalov/Moscow CO/cond. Barshai   HMV ASD631*

VAUGHAN WILLIAMS, Ralph
Concerto (1943)
Rothwell/LSO/cond. Barbirolli   HMV BLP1078*
Williams/Bournemouth SO/cond. Berglund
HMV ASD3127*

VIVALDI, Antonio
Concerto, Op. 7, Nos. 1, 7, P331, P334
Holliger/I Musici   Philips 6700 100*
Il Cimento dell'Armonica e dell'Invenzione, Op. 8, Nos. 9, 12
Pierlot/I Solisti Veneti/cond. Scimone   Erato STU70680(3)*
(No. 9 only:)
Gomberg/New York PO/cond. Bernstein   CBS SBRG72243*
Concerto in C, P41
Caroldi/Accedemici di Milano/cond. Santi   Turnabout 34025
Concerto in F, P259
Holliger/Dresden Staatskapelle/cond. Negri
Philips 6500 413*
Gomberg/New York PO/cond. Bernstein
Columbia MS-6131
Concerto in D minor for two oboes, P302
Duchom, Hihule/Ars Rediviva/cond. Muchlinger
Supraphon SUAST50967*
Caroldi, Alvarosi/Milano Virtuosi/cond. Santi   Vox 513120

The Oboe

Concerto in A minor, P42
Holliger/I Musici   Philips 6500 044*
Lardot/Vienna Solisten/cond. Böttcher   Van. 2138
Concerto in D minor, P43
Sutcliffe/Virtuosi of England/cond. Davison   CFP163*
Shulman/New York Sinfonia/cond. Goberman
     Odyssey 32166214
Concerto in C, P50
Holliger/I Musici   Philips 6500 044*
Krilov/New York Sinfonia/cond. Goberman
     Odyssey 32160214
Concerto in A minor, P80
Schaftlein/Vienna Concertus Musicus/cond. Harnoncourt
     Telefunken AW641961*

Piano and Wind

BEETHOVEN, Ludwig van
Quintet in E flat, Op. 16
Panhofer/Vienna Octet   Decca SDD256*
Paris Wind Ensemble   Nonesuch 71054
     London 6494
Ashkenazy/London Wind Soloists   Philips 6500 326*
Haebler/Bamberg Wind Quartet   Philips 6500 326*
Demus, members of Berlin PO   DG2720 015*
Gieseking/Philharmonia Wind Quartet
     Columbia 33CX1322*

MOZART, Wolfgang Amadeus
Quintet in E flat, K452
Panhofer/Vienna Octet   Decca SDD289*
Ashkenazy/London Wind Soloists   London 6494
Horsley, Brain, et al.   Sera. 60073
Gieseking/Philharmonia Wind Quartet
     Columbia 33CX1322*
Gulda/Vienna Philharmonic Wind Group   DG 138638*

POULENC, Francis
Trio for Flute, Oboe, and Piano
Melos Ensemble   HMV ASD2506*
Sextet (or Sextuor for piano and ww quintet)
Poulenc/Philadelphia Wind Quintet   CSP AMS-6213
Trio for oboe, bassoon, and piano (1926)
Melos Ensemble   Ang. S-36586

RIMSKY-KORSAKOV, Nicolai
Quintet in B flat
Vienna Octet   London STS-15308

Oboe and Harp or Harpsichord

BACH, Carl Philipp Emmanuel
Solo in G minor, Wq 135
  H. Holliger, U. Holliger   Philips SAL3773*

BACH, Johann Sebastian
Sonata in G minor (alternative version of B minor flute
      sonata, BWV1030)
  Holliger, Jaccottet   Philips 6500 618

COUPERIN, François
Concert No. 9 in E (Il ritratto dell'Amore) from Les Goûts
      réunis for oboe d'amore and harpsichord
  Holliger, Jaccottet   Cervera Philips 6500 618*

HUBER, Klaus
Noctes Intelligibilis Lucis
  Holliger   Philips 6500 202*

KŘENEK, Ernst
Aulokithara for oboe, harp, and tape (1971)
  Ostryniec, Lindquist   Orion 76246

MARAIS, Marin
Couplets on "Les Folies d'Espagne"
  Holliger, Jaccottet   Cervera Philips 6500 618*
  Heinitz, Hamilton   Delos 25403

TELEMANN, Georg Philipp
Der Getreue Music-Meister (Sonata in A minor)
  Sous (Baroque oboe)   DG Archiv 1104 943*

Miscellaneous

BACH, Johann Christian
Quintet in D for flute, oboe, violin, viola, and continuo,
      Op. 11, No. 6
  Collegium Pro Arte   OLS182*
Quintet in F for flute, oboe, violin, viola, and continuo,
      Op. 22, No. 2
  Collegium Pro Arte   OLS182*
  Concentus Musicus   AS641062*

BEETHOVEN, Ludwig van
Trio for two oboes and cor anglais, Op. 87
  Pngracz, Toth, Eisenbacher   Hungaroton SLPX11565*
  Casier, François, Baudo   Nonesuch 71025

231

The Oboe

HAYDN, Joseph
  Divertimenti (two oboes, two horns, two bassoons)
  London Wind Soloists/cond. Brymer   London STS-15078

HOLLIGER, Heinz
  Trio for oboe (cor ang), viola, and harp
  H. Holliger, U. Holliger, Collot   Philips 6500 202*

HOLST, Gustav
  Terzetto for flute, oboe, and viola (1924)
  soloists under Imogen Holst   Argo ZRG-5497

PROKOFIEV, Sergei
  Quintet, Op. 39 (ob cl vln vla db)
  Berlin Philharmonic Octet   DG139 309
  Melos Ensemble   Oiseau S-267

Index

Albert family, 22
America,
  tone quality, 87
Anglesey,
  tune 'Pibgorn', 11
Aristotle, 45
  on auloi, 9
  on 'zengos', 7, 8
Articulation and attack, 76–81
  double-tonguing, 78, 79, 81
  triple-tonguing, 78–9
Athenaeum, 23
Attack, *see* Articulation and attack
Aulos, 7, 8, 9
  player of, 8
  windbag variant, 11
Austria, 52
  oboe characteristics, 19
  tone quality, 87
Avison, Charles, 129

Bach Choir, 24
  foundation, 23
Bach, C. P. E., 24, 102, 105, 110,
    114, 119, 128, 129, 152
  on performers, 133
Bach, J. S., 1, 15, 16, 24, 98, 99,
    110, 115, 124, 131, 132–3, 146
  B minor Mass, 22, 23, 25
  Brandenburg Concerti, 131
  Brandenburg Concerto No. 1, 131
  Cantata No. 37, 15
  Goldberg Variations, 111
  Oboe d'Amore Concerto, 160
  Orchestral Suites, 110, 115, 116
  St. John Passion, 23
  St. Matthew Passion, 23, 24
  Suite No. 1 in C, 106, 111, 113,
    132
  Suite No. 3, 116
  Suite No. 4, 105, 110, 115, 116
Baines, Anthony, 8, 9, 11, 18, 101
Bannister, John, 99
  'The Sprightly Companion', 14,
    99
Baroque music, playing, 97–133
  modern editions, 102–3
  ornaments, 107–17

problem of, 97–8
  style, 103–7
  tone quality, 98–100
Barret, Apollon, 18, 21, 22
  Tutors, 21
Bartók, Béla, 143
Bartolozzi, Bruno, 166, 173
Bate, Philip, 13, 101
Batten, Joe, 162
Beethoven, 16, 17, 25, 99, 151, 152,
    153, 159, 182
  'Ah, Perfido', Op. 65, 25
  Choral Fantasy, 25
  Eroica Symphony, 152
  'Fidelio', 25, 149–50
  Fifth Symphony, 25, 151
  Fourth Piano Concerto, 25
  lack of recognition, 25–6
  'Leonora' No. 3 Overture, 153
  Mass in C, 25
  Ninth Symphony, 17, 81, 151, 156
  Pastoral Symphony, 151
  Seventh Symphony, 151
  Sixth Symphony, 25
  use of oboe for characterization,
    151–2
  Violin Concerto, 99
Belgium,
  oboe-making, 22
Bellini, Vincenzo, 152
Bennett, Richard Rodney,
  Oboe Concerto, 175
Berio,
  'Epiphonie', 184
  'Sequenza VII', 171, 172, 184
Berlioz, 18, 20, 26, 149, 154, 156
  as conductor, 156
  'Fantastic Symphony', 18, 25, 153
  on cor anglais, 154
  on Indian oboes, 5–6, 169
  orchestra, 135
  Scène aux Champs, 153, 154
  'Treatise', 24, 152–3
Besozzis, the, 134, 144
Blackwood, African, 35, 51
Boehm, Theobald, 18
  work on oboe, 22
Boethius, 10

Boughton, Rutland, 159
Bozza, Eugène,
'14 Studies in Karnatic Modes', 70
Brahms, 18, 153, 159
Symphony No. 1, 83, 84, 85
Violin Concerto, 90, 93
Brearley, T., 44, 52
Breath control, 32, 53, 70–2
exercises, 74–5
inhaling, 72–3
sustaining sound while
breathing-in, 169–70
British Museum,
Elgin pipes, 8–9
Britten, Benjamin,
'Six Metamorphoses after Ovid',
182, 183
Brod, Henri, 20, 26
Brueghel the Elder, Pieter,
The Peasant Dance, 11
The Peasant Wedding, 11
Brussels, 23
Musée de Peinture, 12
Buffet, Louis Auguste, 22
Burney, Dr Charles,
History of Music, 24, 103
on Bach, 24
visits C. P. E. Bach, 103

Calcutta, 5
Cambert, Robert,
'Pomone', 14
Cambini, G. G., 135
Cassiodorus, 10
Castiglioni, Niccolo,
'Alef', 179
Cherubini, Luigi, 20
Chopin, 116
Chords, see Multiphonic procedures
Chrysander, Friedrich, 119
Classical music, playing, 134–48
inserting a cadenza, 140–3
orchestral technique, 143–8
Commonwealth, Cromwell's, 13
Cor anglais, 15–16, 20, 23, 24–5, 154
reeds, 48–9
tone quality, 93–4
Cornett, 12
Couperin, François, 102, 104, 106,
116, 132, 133, 151
Craxton, Janet, 43
Crook, 49
Crusades,
introduce Arabian oboe to
Europe, 10

Danican, see Philidor, Michel
Delius,
'La Calinda', 91, 93
Donington, Robert, 104, 107, 110,
118

Dulcian, 12
Dynamics, 81–6

Edinburgh,
Usher Hall, 160
Edison Bell, 162
Editorial faults, 102–3, 142
Egypt,
ancient flute, 7
New Kingdom, 6
oboes in, 6
Einstein, Alfred, 135, 136
Electronics, 166, 181
Elgar, Sir Edward, 159–60
Suite for Oboe, 160
Embellishment, see Extemporization
and embellishment
Embouchure, 32, 48, 52–3, 54–8, 98
and reed, 167–9
England,
slow development of 19th century
oboe, 22–3
Esterhazy, Prince,
court of, 144
Extemporization and embellishment,
118–33

Ferlendis, Alessandro, 139
Fétis, François Joseph, 7
'History of Music', 7
Field of the Cloth of Gold, 11
Fingering technique, special
characteristics of basic, 61–8
Fischer, G. C., 99
Florence,
Egyptian Museum, 7
Flute, 7, 22
Egyptian, 7
flute-à-bec, 7
France,
Conservatoire founded, 19
innovations in oboe, 18, 20–22
style of playing, 103, 104–7
tone quality, 87
Franck, César, 153
Furtwängler, Wilhelm, 52

Galant style, 129, 137
Garnier, François Joseph, 98
Geminiani, Francesco, 129, 131
Germany,
French designs adopted, 18–19
oboe sound, 19
style of playing, 103–4
Gillet, George, 21–2
'Gillet model' oboe, 22, 171, 175
Gleditsch, 1
Glissandi, 175–6
Goossens, Eugene,
Concerto, 159
Goossens, Leon, 11

Grainger, Percy, 159
Grattan-Cooke, 22, 23

Halévy, Jacques,
  'The Jewess', 25
Handel, 99, 111
  'Acis and Galatea', 117
  admiration of oboe, 118
  B flat Oboe Concerto, 117
  G minor Oboe Concerto, 114, 117
  'Messiah', 132
  Pastoral Symphony from
    'Messiah', 111, 112
  Six Sonatas for two oboes, 118
  Sonata in C minor, 119, 120–29
Hanslick, Eduard, 24
Harmonics, 170–3
  double, 179–81
Harvard Dictionary of Music, 99
Hautbois, see Oboe
Hawkins, John, 144
Haydn, 138, 144, 145, 146
  'Harmony' Mass, 145
  'Le Coq', 145
  'Le Midi' Symphony No. 7, 145
  'London' Symphonies, 146
  Sinfonia Concertante Op. 84, 146
  Symphony No. 11, 144
  Symphony No. 96, 145, 146
  use of oboist, 138, 145
Heckel, Wilhelm, 26
Heckelphone, 26
Helmholtz, H. L. F. von, 166
Henry VIII,
  collection of recorders, 12
Henry Wood Promenade Concerts,
  closed down by bombing, 159
Hoffmann, E. T. A., 17
  Beethovens Instrumentalmusik, 149
Holliger, Heinz, 171
  'Cardiophonie', 181
  'Siebengesang', 181, 182
Holst, Gustav,
  'The Planets' Suite, 26
Homer,
  'Iliad', 7
Hotteterre, Jacques, 97, 99, 102,
  105, 107, 109, 114, 116, 131
  *Principles of the Flute, Recorder
    and Oboe*, 107, 108
Hotteterre, Jean, 13, 18
  designs oboe proper, 14
  workshop, 14
Huber, Klaus, 173, 176, 183
  'Noctes', 175, 176

Iceland,
  Reykjavik Orchestra, 51
Intonation, 163–4
Italy,
  style of playing, 103

Kang-Hi, Emperor, 6

Lasocki, David, 109
Lavigne, A. J., 22
Le Gros, Joseph, 135
Lenon, H. G., 24
Lipowsky, F. J., 136, 138
  'Baierisches Musik-Lexicon', 135
  on Ramm, 135–6
London,
  Covent Garden, 21
  Queen's Hall Orchestra, 87
  Royal Albert Hall, 153
Lorée, François, 21, 26
Louis XIII, 13
Louis XIV, 13
Lully, Jean-Baptiste, 13, 14, 104, 106
  ballets, 14

Maestro-conductor, rise of, 156
Mahler, Gustav, 143
Mallilon, 23
Malsch, 18
Mann, Thomas, 155
Mannheim Orchestra, 135
Martini, 144
Marx, Josef, 99
Masson, P. M., 110
Mattheson, Johann, 99
Mendelssohn, 153
  as conductor, 156
Meyerbeer,
  'Les Huguenots', 24
Mozart, 1, 19, 129, 134–5, 136–7,
  138, 139, 143, 144
  'Così fan Tutte' Overture, 64
  G minor Symphony, No. 25, 144
  G minor Symphony, No. 40, 144–5
  'Idomeneo', 136
  Oboe Concerto, 81, 84, 139–40
  Piano Concerto K. 491, 146–8
  Quartet for Oboe and Strings,
    135, 136, 137–9
  Sinfonia Concertante for Violin
    and Viola, 92, 93, 134–5
Mozart, Leopold, 144
Multiphonic procedures, 177–9
  homogeneous chords, 178
  homogeneous chords mixed with
    single notes, 179
Musette, 14
Musical World, 23

Nagasuram, 6
Naples,
  Museo Nazionale, 10
  pifferari, 111, 112
Nietzsche, 155
Note-bending, 173

Oboe,
alto oboe, *see* Oboe d'amore
Arabian, 10
at Sumerian royal funeral, 5
baroque, 14–15, 97 *et seq.*
bass oboe, 26
Burmese, 6
Chaldaean (from Ur), 5
Chinese, 6
classical, 17–18, 134
Conservatoire system, 21–2, 171, 175
dynamics, 81–6
Egyptian, 6
Etruscan, 8, 9, 10
extension of note holes, 19
Graeco-Roman, 7–10
Indian, 5, 6
introduction of mechanized, 17–27
Lorée, 26, 27, 136, 157
maintenance, 50–3
Mexican, 6
Mongolian, 6
muting, 52
oboe proper designed, 14
oiling, 51
orchestral role in nineteenth century, 18
producing first sound, 53–4
revival under Louis XIV, 13–14
survival in Dark Ages, 10, 11
tenor oboe, *see* Cor anglais
tone quality, 86–7, 98–100
Triébert, 18, 26, 27, 136
vibrato, 87–93, 98, 101, 109, 173, 174
windbag oboe, 11
Oboe da caccia, *see* Cor anglais
Oboe d'amore, 15, 16, 23, 24, 160
reed, 49
Orchomenus, Lake, 8
Ornaments, 107–17
accent (18th century), 109, 117, 176
appoggiatura, 107–8, 110, 123, 128, 129
battement, 109, 123
flattement, 109, 174
messa di voce, 109, 123, 134, 152
trill (shake), 107, 116–17, 128, 129, 181
Otou/ottu, 5, 6, 169
Otto Langay Tutor, 20

Pan, 2, 89
Paris,
Concerts Spirituels, 135
Great Exhibition, 5
Opera, 14
Paris Conservatoire, 21
approved design of oboe, 21–2,

171, 175
founded, 19
Philadelphia, 87
University Museum, 5
Philidor, Michel, 13
Piatigorsky, Gregor, 163
Pibgorn, 11
Pinder, Robert, 100
Polworth, Lord, 118
Pommer, *see* Shawm, bass
Pompeii,
auloi from, 9–10
Posture, 58–61
Poulenc, Francis,
Trio for Oboe, Bassoon and Piano, 63
Praetorius,
on shawms, 12, 99
Prelleur, Peter, 98
Projection, 32
Prokofiev,
'Peter and the Wolf', 82
Punto, Giovanni, 135
Purcell, Henry, 14, 100–1, 107, 113
'Come ye Sons of Art', 100

Quacking, 78, 88
Quantz, J. J., 97, 98, 105, 107, 108, 110, 113, 116, 117, 119, 123, 129
Guide to the Flute, 105, 108, 109
on ornamentation, 118–19
on performers, 133
'On Playing the Flute', 102
Quarter-tones, 174

Raguenet, François, 99
Ramm, Friedrich, 1, 135, 137, 138, 144, 145
Ravel, 89
'Daphnis and Chloe', 88, 89
Recording, 161–2
Reed, 31–49, 164
barrel (or easel) for, 36, 49
binding, 40, 42
binding thread for, 36, 49
cane for, 35–6
cor anglais, 48–9
cutting block for, 34
embouchure and, 167–9
faulty, 45–8
fibre-glass, 164–5
goldbeater's skin for, 36, 45, 49
gouging, 37–8, 49
knife for, 32
mandrel for, 35
oboe d'amore, 49
pliers and scissors for, 36–7, 49
reed-making equipment, 32–7
ruler for, 36
scraping, 42–5

scraping tongue (or plaque) for,
    34–5
shaper for, 37, 49
shaping, 38–40
sharpening stone for knife, 34
shawm, 13
staples for, 35, 49
too hard, 45–6, 52
too soft, 46–7, 52
'zengos', 7, 8
Reichardt, J. F., 25
Renaissance,
    proliferation of woodwind
        instruments, 11
Reynolds, Charles, 52, 169
Richter, 169
Rimsky-Korsakov, 146
Romantic music, playing of, 149–57
Rossini, 1
    'The Barber of Seville', 80
    'The Silken Ladder' overture, 79
Roxburgh, Edwin, 97, 166

Sachs, Curt, 6
Sackbut, 12
Sallaert, Antoine,
    'La Procession des Pucelles du
        Sablon', 12
Sallantin, Antoine, 19
Salzburg, 136
Sammartini, Giuseppe, 144
Sanayi, 6
Scales, 69–70
Schopenhauer,
    on music, 154–5
Schubert,
    'Unfinished Symphony', 92, 93
Schumann, 154
    Cello Concerto, 162
Schürmann, G. K.,
    'Ludwig der Fromme', 15
Scott, Cyril, 159
    Oboe Concerto, 159
Sellner, Josef,
    'Oboeschule', 18
Shawm, 12–13, 99
    bass, 12
    becomes obsolete, 14
    folk-shawm, 11
    Persian, 10
Sibelius,
    'Swan of Tuonela', 82
Smith, H., 24
Socrates,
    on the auletes, 9
Sophocles, 9
Spohr, Louis, 152
Sprenkle and Ledet, 86
Statius,
    on the tibia, 10

Stockhausen,
    'Stimmung', 172
    Wind Quintet 'Zeitmasse', 182,
        183
Strauss, Richard,
    'Elektra', 26
    Oboe Concerto, 32, 158–9
    'Salome', 26
Stravinsky, 58
    'Pulcinella', 57
    'Rite of Spring', 93, 94, 176
Surna, see Shawm
Syrinx, 2
Syrinx, the, 7, 8

Tabuteau, 87
Talbot, James, 14–15, 16, 110
Tarquinia, 10
Tartini, Giuseppe, 118
Teacher, the, 53
Telemann, G. P., 15, 102, 133
    'Der Sieg der Schönheit', 15
    Sonata in A minor, 117
Tenoroon, 22, 23
Theophrastus,
    on cane for auloi, 8
Thirty Years War, 13
Tinctoris, 11
Tomassini, Luigi, 145
Tomb of the Leopards, 8
Tone,
    quality, 86–7, 98–100
    recording and tone quality, 161
    reed and, 31
    rolling, 176–7
Tongue,
    double-tonguing, 78, 79, 81
    flutter-tonguing, 176
    reed and, 31–2
    triple-tonguing, 78–9
Tovey, Sir Donald, 160, 161, 165
Triébert, F., 21
Triébert, Guillaume, 9, 20, 26
    transforms oboe, 20–21

Ur, 5

Vaughan Williams, Ralph, 159
    Concerto, 159, 161, 162
Verdi, 6
    composes 'Aida', 7
    on Fétis, 7
Vibrato, 87–93, 98, 101, 173, 174
    combined fast and slow, 92–3
    eighteenth-century, 109
    fast, 92
    medium, 91
    no vibrato, 88–9
    slow, 90–91
Vogt, Auguste-Gustave, 19, 20

Wagner, 19, 26, 52, 153, 154, 156, 157, 158, 165
  as conductor, 156–7
  'Parsifal', 165
  romantic spirit personified, 155
  'Tristan and Isolde', 155–6, 169

Weidemann, K. F., 118
Wind orchestra, sixteenth-century, 12
Woolley, Sir Leonard, 5

Zamr, *see* Shawm